CW00540907

Perseverance

JOURNEY to ALASKA

Perseverance

JOURNEY to ALASKA

STEVEN HARRISON

atmosphere press

© 2023 Steven Harrison

Published by Atmosphere Press

Cover design by Senhor Tocas

Map in front by Samantha Portnoy

No part of this book may be reproduced without permission from the author except in brief quotations and in reviews.

Atmospherepress.com

CONTENTS

PART ONE

PART TWO

PART THREE

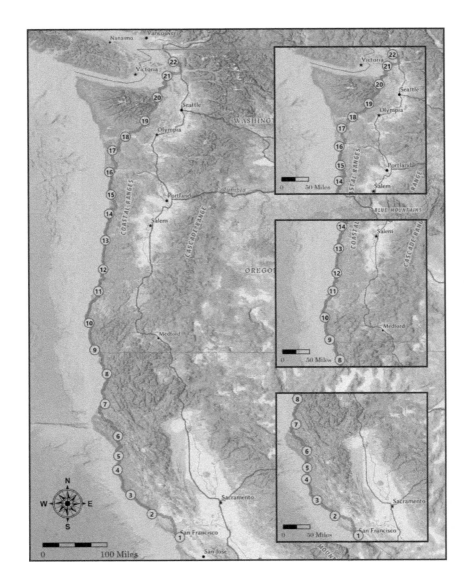

PREFACE

In 2018, I started writing articles for Quora. I wrote a variety of articles but focused mainly on running and cycling, two subjects I have extensive life experience in. Later that year, I received a check from Quora for my articles. I was now a professional writer. I celebrated the event by taking myself out to dinner. I spent more on dinner than my first check. I did not care; I was a professional writer. I have been writing ever since. I added becoming a published author to my bucket list that night.

I have written hundreds of articles over the past five years and several short sci-fi stories. When I left on my ride for Alaska, I was working on a sci-fi trilogy approaching 85,000 words and three-quarters complete. I set that aside to document my ride up the West Coast. My original plan was to write a travel guide for e-bike riders. Every night in front of a campfire, I sat with my laptop, writing my notes for the day. I focused on the subjects pertinent to recharging my electric bike and campsites along the way. As my ride evolved from accomplishing a bucket list item—seeing my fiftieth state—to a completely life-changing experience, my subject matter changed as well. I started writing more extensively about what I was going through.

By the time I hit the halfway point on my journey, I knew I was not going home. My writing took a sharp left turn at that point. I wrote from a different perspective. I was not writing a travel guide; I was writing a life guide. Perspective is important for any writer. If you are writing about changing your life, there is no better perspective than to lead by example. I took to the challenge and wrote from the heart. I wrote about the experience, the thought process, the challenges, and the dream of a better life. I transformed those daily notes into the story you are about to read. Enjoy.

Steven Harrison
March 25, 2023

PART ONE

PRELUDE to a RIDE

I planned this trip for four months. In mid-February, I had an epiphany that getting back in shape after Covid-19 might be a good idea. I started riding every day. Some days, only 10 or 15 miles. On short days, I did sprints. I'd ride from downtown San Francisco to Ocean Beach and back; the 16-mile trip took 42 minutes. That is hard, even on an e-bike. I increased the distance, and soon I was riding 26 miles to Taco Bell in Linda Mar, eating a chalupa, and racing back to the city. I timed how quickly I could get from Union Square across the Golden Gate Bridge (GGB). By the end of March, I was up at 6 am each day, racing across the GGB to sprint the Marin Headlands. The next month, to the top of Mount Tamalpais.

I challenged my previous time. I circled Paradise Drive around the Tiburon Peninsula and back to the city. By the end of April, I was riding 50 to 60 miles in three hours, then grabbing a Jamba Juice and hitting the gym. At the end of May, I decided to test my mettle. I planned a trip to Yosemite National Park. I spent time and money fitting out my bike and trailer. I increased the size and capacity of the bike trailer.

I spent hours agonizing how to make it stronger so it could

5

hold more things. I overpacked on my trip. By the end of the second day, I was giving food away. The third day, I crested the pass on Highway 120, at 6,121 feet in elevation. I cursed myself for bringing heavy tools, extra food, clothing, laptop, iPad, and iPhone. I questioned why I did not bring my printer, TV, and Xbox. I learned that too much weight makes for a painful ride, not a pleasant one. I had a great time in Yosemite even for one day. On Sunday, I headed home. It took two days for me to get back.

I learned charging my e-bike could be problematic. Yosemite is not e-bike friendly. I learned how to unplug a Coke machine to charge my bike in Yosemite—but don't tell housekeeping, as they are still wondering why their Cokes were warm Sunday morning. I made wrong turns and poor decisions, but when I left for Alaska, I had learned hard lessons.

Pack lighter, plan better, follow the map, and only bring enough food for 48 hours. There are plenty of stores willing to gouge you no matter where you are. Another benefit of not carrying much food and water: it gives you an excuse to stop at restaurants and charge your bike. Stopping every two hours to top off your battery is good and bad. It breaks up your ride into short, manageable segments but also makes a 60-mile ride a 10-hour day. A 50-mile ride could be four hours, leaving the rest of the day to play at the beach, the lake, or river. A 60-mile ride towing a trailer took 10 hours. Recharging takes time.

The battery life on your e-bike diminishes quickly with elevation gain. Monitoring your battery use so you do not lose power is critical. Learning the basics of how, what, where, and when to charge can make your day easy. You might plan well, only to find the town you planned to have lunch in is not a town but a gas station. Asking "Is there a place I can charge my battery for an hour?" will get you a grunt and a stare. That is not an ideal way to have a good time. It happens when you least expect it, so learning your limits is a good idea.

I got home from Yosemite on Memorial Day and went to work Tuesday morning. I was a bit sore, but proud of my five-day adventure. Two days out, one day there, and two days back. I learned what I needed to learn. Use more sunblock, carry twice as much water, leave 30 pounds of groceries at home. No power tools were necessary. Sunglasses help keep bugs out of your eyes. Having a rain fly for your tent helps you stay dry. Climbing the Sierra Mountains on any bike is a lot of work. I also learned I could do it. I could ride 65 miles over rough terrain in a day. Given time to charge and the desire, my body could manage the ride. I immediately made a list of the things I would need for Alaska, which was becoming not a dream, but a reality.

The RIDE

I planned to leave August 1, 2021. I gave myself six weeks to train and plan my ride. Like all good plans, these were subject to change. Impetus for changing my start date from August 1 to June 11 was significant. A serious deterioration in the quiet enjoyment of my residence made leaving a good idea. Death threats from neighbors tend to do that. I paid my rent for the next two months and left the next day.

I worked nonstop during Covid-19 lockdown. San Francisco shut down earlier than most cities. As an essential worker in a critical capacity, it had been impossible to vacation earlier. I worked as a development associate for a nonprofit delivering free groceries to senior citizens and disabled persons in San Francisco. When the city finally settled back to normal, the option to take a month off was available. Not desirable, but doable. I told my boss I needed a month off and left the next day at 4 am.

Day 1
Friday, June 11, 2021, 4 am

Day one. I could not sleep. I had gone to bed at 10 pm with the intention of sleeping till 5 am and hitting the road at 6 am. It did not happen that way. Call it jitters or nervous energy, but I was up at 2 am, and the thought of going back to bed was not in the cards. I had packed the night before, so I went through my checklist once again. I drank the strongest coffee known to mankind, took my vitamins, drank a protein smoothie, checked my list again, showered, shaved, and changed into my riding gear. It was 3:30 am. I dragged my fully loaded trailer down to the lobby. The desk clerk gave me a funny look, then she nodded off.

I brought my bike downstairs and hooked the trailer to the bike. I looked at the clock on the wall—ten minutes to four. I went back upstairs, looked around, went to the bathroom, and locked the door behind me. It was 4 am. The city was still dark, but plenty of streetlight. The first 40 miles were up and over the Golden Gate Bridge, through Sausalito, Mill Valley, Corte Madera, Larkspur, Ross, San Anselmo, Fairfax, and out to Olema on Sir Francis Drake Blvd. I grew up in Marin and knew the roads well, so the dark did not bother me.

I crossed the Golden Gate Bridge at 4:30 am and did not pass a single car until I got to Larkspur. Two deer crossed the road on Bridgeway in Sausalito, giving me the stink eye. I kept riding. I saw three more deer in San Anselmo, but they did not appear to be bothered with my early morning ride. By 8 am, I was in Olema and needed to refuel—both my body and battery.

My first stop was the campground/post office in Olema. There is an electrical outlet near the laundry room next to the post office. I plugged in and made breakfast in the day-use area. I realized I'd left my book at home and made a note to pick up something to read. I waited two hours for the bike to charge halfway, and shortly before 10 am, I was back on the road.

I wanted to put as much distance between me and the city as possible. The road was smooth with a shoulder. I rode Highway 1 through Inverness, Marshall, and Dillon Beach. I stopped in Tomales, had breakfast and coffee. I used the deli's outlet to top off my battery while I ate. I rode through Valley Ford into Bodega. The road is full of short, steep hills, like a roller coaster. By the time I got to Bodega, my battery was 15%. I stopped in town for two hours and took a nap while my bike charged at a casino. I thanked the proprietor, heading north again. I realized I was extremely tired and pulled into the resort town of Bodega Bay. I asked the nearest hotel how much rooms were. I choked; they quoted me $550 for the night. I politely declined and got back on my bike. The next spot quoted me $160, which was more than I wanted to spend, but I had ridden 87 miles and was dead tired. I paid the fee, took a shower, and asked the woman at the front desk where I could get fish and chips.

She pointed me in the right direction. Luckily, the place was close, had outdoor seating, and was quick and easy. I felt peaceful, content, and sleepy. I'd slept four hours the night before and had ridden 87 miles. I slept well that night but wanted an early start. Everybody warned me about "traveling north." Everybody rides south due to prevailing winds. One way to minimize the wind is to ride early and be off the road by noon. Riding a thousand miles into the wind can be daunting—even with an electric bike.

Day 2
Saturday, June 12, 2021

I was up at 4 am, on the road at 5:30 am. I'd had trouble with the Burley Bee trailer the previous day, the sides rubbing on the tires. The morning was beautiful, just a little overcast, but nice. I spent two hours riding hard. With a fully charged battery, I made good time, arriving at Fort Ross with a stomach growling and the battery waning. I rolled into the park and passed the Ranger Station. The Park Ranger was setting up for the day. There was a day use fee; I smiled and waved as I rode by. She waved back, so I figured my smile paid the fee.

I found a picnic table and dropped off my food. I scouted Fort Ross for electricity and found what I was looking for on the side of the building. I walked back to my table and made oatmeal. I chopped up a Larabar and put it in my oatmeal. It tasted better with the Larabar.

After breakfast, the cleaning crew showed up at Fort Ross visitor center. I was the only person there; the cleaning girl waved to me and I waved back. I went for a walk and left my bike. The Ranger and cleaning crew would watch my bike. I went to see Fort Ross.

Fort Ross is a state park that pays real and recreated homage to the original Russian fort. It served the Russian community living in Alaska. The Alaskan territory did not have enough arable land to grow grain and raise cattle, so they built Fort Ross to trade with indigenous people and the Mexican population. There are remnants of the old fort and recreated buildings that are interesting and worth the hike.

There is a windmill with unique Russian innovations. The Russian plains windmill, built with few nails, is a marvel of seventeenth century engineering. I recommend stopping at Fort Ross. If you get there before they are officially open, try paying with a smile. It worked for me.

With my battery at 80%, I packed my food and got back in the saddle, heading up Highway 1. The road has a tiny shoulder, but I continued taking in the beauty of the Northern California coast. I limited pictures to epic shots. The only problem was the whole ride was epic shots.

I rolled into Gualala on the Sonoma-Mendocino border, scouting campgrounds on the southern side of town. I buzzed into the campground at 2 pm. I had ridden 60 miles, good enough to check out the campground. It was self-pay; I saw when I stopped and read the sign. I used one of the envelopes to pay $5. That was better than $160 the night before. I inserted my cash and proceeded to the campground.

The first thing I see is the Camp Host and a sign saying, "Campground Full." Oh boy, I just paid big bucks for a site; I was going to get turned out. I rolled to the Camp Host and smiled. She smiled back. I was in luck, my smiles worked like Bitcoins. She waved me through and said I was her first hiker/biker of the day. She smiled, telling me to take HB2, a good site. I made my way to HB2 and found a slice of heaven next to Gualala Creek. I stripped out of my biking clothes and went for a dip in the creek. A few kayakers rowed by in convoy and tried to run me over. The creek was in a drought, about 10 feet wide and moving at the ferocious rate of 1 mph. The train of kayakers scootched by me three inches above the rocky bottom. The bigger bodies had to get out and carry across the shallow parts.

It looked like fun even if the river was crawling and very shallow. I asked where I could rent a kayak; they pointed to the bridge, a half mile away. I finished cooling down, ate lunch, and went to find the kayak rental. I got diverted in my adventure looking for the kayak rental and ended up at the beach. I stopped at the golf course. I did not play, but watched a few couples play through. I talked to a ranger and lost track of time. I needed to charge my bike and make dinner.

I rode across the bridge into town and saw the kayak station. Tomorrow, there would be another kayak station. It looked fun, but it was 6pm and the day was rapidly closing. The sun wasn't setting but my eyelids were drooping. I bought a steak and a couple of nonalcoholic beers for dinner.

Back at the campsite, I asked the camp host if I could use the electrical outlet in the bathroom. She responded, "You can charge right here." The camp host came with electrical benefits. My smiles must be worth a Bitcoin. Not only did I have a place to charge, but I also had a babysitter for my bike. I hiked back to my site, started a fire for my steak and potatoes. I wrapped two potatoes in tinfoil and threw them into the fire. Twenty minutes later, I closed the grill over my fire ring and spread hot coals under the steak; fifteen minutes later, I had a meal fit for a biker. The ranger came by, and I offered her a nonalcoholic beer. She said she was still on duty; we both laughed. I had a second beer. I was asleep at 8:30 pm; it must have been the beer.

Day 3
Sunday, June 13, 2021

I'd planned to get up at 4 am, but I rolled over, turned off the alarm, then got out of my sleeping bag at 5:30 am. I made breakfast and coffee, packed my tent and gear, picked up my bike from the host, and headed down the highway. The sun was coming up over the coastal mountains. I made good time and arrived in Point Arena before 9 am. I was down to 50%, so I stopped at the Last Café in Point Arena and ordered a Denver omelet. I still had a lot of miles in front of me. My goal: the Russian Gulch campground just north of Mendocino.

I decided to let my bike charge, taking a walk out to the Point Arena Lighthouse. I walked across the street to a gate leading to a cow pasture. There was a trail to the lighthouse. I walked a quarter mile when I noticed a cow following me. I was not sure why. I looked back a few minutes later and there was another cow following me. I could see more cows off to the side and some in front of me. I walked a mile towards the lighthouse; I now had ten cows following me. Before I hiked another half mile, I had 20 cows following me. They did not try to get any closer than 30 yards. I checked my pockets and wondered what the cows wanted.

I took pictures of the lighthouse; it was still another mile away. I turned around, heading back. The cows turned and followed. This was getting strange. I was by myself in the middle of a cow pasture with 30 cows following me around. I started laughing and talked to the cows. They liked that and came within 20 yards. I dropped down a small rise and was now coming up the hill where I could see the restaurant. I saw a farmer walking the fence line. He was looking for a break in the fence line. He looked up and saw me walking through the field with 30 cows following me. They started bellowing. The cows needed eyeglasses; it was a case of mistaken identity. I could feel them pick up the pace as we approached the farmer. I smiled and said hello, making for the gate in the fence. I felt him staring at me as I walked by; I said nothing, I just smiled. Even cows appreciate a Bitcoin smile.

Heading down Highway 1 at speed, I wanted to make the Russian gulch before 4 pm. I used more battery than I should have. The shoulder on the highway is nonexistent. That is not good for a biker towing a trailer. Cars coming around blind turns and sharp hills could not see me. I put the bike in medium power, and for the next 20 miles, I pushed it at 25 mph. This area is dangerous if not approached right. At noon, I needed to rest, the battery down to 28%. I was 30 miles from my destination.

I pulled into Elk, scanning the area for electricity. It was hot, so I found shade and an outlet behind the post office. I bought two Gatorades and found a mini library. I borrowed *The Girl with the Dragon Tattoo*. I sat at the post office in Elk, reading my book. I greeted people as they came to check on their mail. I sat in front of the post office for an hour. Tourists needing directions stopped and asked questions. I told them I was the mayor of Elk (population 208). I said it with a big smile, but they missed the sarcasm, so I just played along. I gave them good advice; I knew the answers to their questions.

My battery at 60%, I resigned my mayorship and said goodbye to Elk, California. I liked being the mayor, even for an hour. I felt bad not having a book to replace the one I borrowed.

Please donate a book when you pass through Elk. We cannot let it be known that the mayor made off with a Dragon Tattoo without recompense. Thank you.

I rode fast and hard for the next 21 miles. I arrived in Albion, California, at 2:30 pm. I needed to charge again. I wanted to make the Russian Gulch Campground, which was 10 hilly miles away. When you ride fast, you burn the battery quickly. You can travel slower and pedal harder, but pulling a trailer in the afternoon wind is not productive. My battery had 18%, so I pulled into the Little River Inn. I did not know they had a golf course. I chatted with Maria in housekeeping, who allowed me to charge my bike at the laundry facilities. I offered a few kind words in Spanish, and she promised to watch my bike. This allowed me to perfect the best way to charge an e-bike.

I headed to the golf pro shop, rented clubs, and got a bucket of balls. After shaking off the cobwebs in my swing, I was driving 225 yards with a three wood, hitting the five iron 175. Down from my normal swing, but my normal was fifteen years ago. I went to play nine and proceeded to play poorly, but I was multitasking. My true aim was charging my bike; playing golf and practicing my putting was a diversionary tactic. I felt good and by the sixth hole, I made par. (My first and only par that day.) Feeling like Tiger Woods on his worst day, I finished the front nine and turned in my rental clubs. Off to find Maria in housekeeping.

I told Maria about my golf prowess and she smiled suspiciously. Knowing my Spanish was rusty, I wondered what I'd said. She laughed; it could not be that bad. She left me to my travels; she had more rooms to clean. I was happy, even though I'd added a 52 to my handicap. For those not in the know, that is a very bad day. Did I care? No, not the slightest. I left the resort with an e-bike charged to 58%, so I had enough juice to power my way through Mendocino to my destination.

I arrived at the Russian Gulch Campground, paying the un-exorbitant fee of $10. I set up my four-man tent, missing the rain fly, under a tree. It started to rain. Oh boy, this was going to be fun. I'd lost my rain fly one night months before when I went on a Covid-19 sabbatical with my then girlfriend. It was a lot of fun (not) but my girlfriend overpacked and there was no room to transport the rain fly home. Recalling unfond memories of a bad situation, I manufactured an impromptu rain fly out of a tarp. Unfortunately, it only covered part of the top and leaked all night. I woke up with my feet in a puddle of water.

My sleeping bag kept me warm, but it was now wet. When stuffed, wet bags gather mold. I did the best I could to dry it and stuffed it anyway. I threw the tent in the trash.

Day 4
Monday, June 14, 2021

I was car camping with a bike. Pulling a trailer allows you to overpack. I did not need a four-man tent. It allowed me to store my bike inside, but this was a luxury I could not afford. I needed two new tires for my trailer, as they were threadbare. For the next week, I would be traveling through an area with limited stores and few bike shops. I woke up late, made coffee. I knew I was riding 15 miles to Fort Bragg. I would wait until 11 am for the bike shop to open.

I charged my bike all night inside the campground bathroom. It was safe; I camped next to the facility. I packed, and now missing a tent, I had room to spare. I left at 7:30 am and passed a camper three sites over from mine. I waved and smiled, having conversed with its residents last night. I put my engine on medium power and zipped down the highway to Fort Bragg. The short fifteen-mile ride took a half hour. I was going the maximum speed of the e-bike, 28 mph. I found the bike shop without trouble. It was in the same building as a coffee shop. I ran into the couple from the campground. They were amazed to see me and asked how I'd traveled that far in the same amount of time it had taken them to drive.

I shrugged; the speed limit is 45 mph. I rode almost 30 mph, so the difference over 15 miles is not much. I found a place inside to charge my bike and sat down. I ordered a chocolate donut and a large cup of coffee. They sold monster-sized chocolate chip cookies. I could not resist, so I sat there early Monday morning eating a huge cookie, charging my e-bike, and texting my friends pictures of me multitasking. They did not appreciate my multitasking skills. You try eating a cookie, drinking coffee, updating your Facebook page, AND charging your e-bike at the same time. This takes a special skill, which I have carefully honed with dedicated practice. Wouldn't you appreciate a picture of a friend in a coffee shop eating a cookie bigger than his head while charging his e-bike on a Monday morning? I did not understand why my friends, chained to their desks, did not find this commendable.

The bike shop opened at 11 am. I sat in the coffee shop for an hour, met some locals. They asked many questions; I answered without any exaggeration. Where was I going? How fast did my e-bike go? How long did a charge last? Where did I start? Answers: I was going to Alaska, it went 35 mph, it lasted all day long, and I started in Fort Lauderdale, Florida. Which is technically true because I was born in Fort Lauderdale. Right? It went 35 mph down a steep hill. It lasted all day if you rode three hours a day. What people focused on was Alaska. I was serious—that was the whole point of my ride. I left San Francisco with the goal of seeing my fiftieth state. I was determined to see its beauty.

When the bike shop opened, I waited patiently for the proprietor before asking a thousand and one questions. He was nice, helpful. I bought two tires, which I put on myself. He let me borrow his foot pump to reassemble the trailer. I thanked him, asking where I could purchase a tent. The camping store was next door. I introduced myself at the camping store and asked another thousand and one questions. I walked out with a beautiful two-man tent that weighed half the amount of the four-man and took up half the space.

I filled the extra space with Gatorade and food. It was 1 pm. The fog had cleared, and the sun was out, but the wind had picked up. I had a fully charged bike. Fueled on chocolate chips, I rode the coast of Northern California. Some days, logistics and weather have more to do with your ride than anything else.

I rode hard for two hours, ending at the KOA in Westport, California. The next 26 miles were over the coastal mountains into Leggett, California. This 26-mile leg was over a 3,000-foot mountain. I was going to need a full battery and all my strength. I decided to call it a day, as I had ridden 38 miles. It did not matter; this was the last place I could charge my bike before I climbed a mountain.

I did not like the $65 fee for electricity at the KOA, and I was sandwiched between two monster five-wheel trailers. I felt like a serf between kings' castles, my tiny two-man tent between million-dollar rigs. It diffused the aura of my new tent. I wanted to show them a real camper. My tiny little tent did not cut the mustard.

The campsite was full of kids, which made me happy. Riding bikes, playing kickball, throwing frisbees, kids being kids. Living in San Francisco, you forget about kids playing in the street, but this was a campground. It was nice to see. I went to the beach, brought my laptop. No internet connection or phone service. It did not matter. The campsite included free wi-fi, but out on the ocean, nada.

I spoke to a guy who was fishing. He caught a bunch of seaweed, twice. I saw his line get dragged; kelp can do that to a hook. It was warm, so I ran and dove into the Pacific Ocean. The freezing cold took my breath away, so I ducked down under a wave and called it a day. Back at camp, I made chili dogs for dinner. I had ice cream from the campground store. An

It's-It for $4 seemed expensive, but it capped a good day. Not much riding, but still a good day. I had an intellectual conversation with the couple camped next to me. The wife was well read, and the husband was a retired rocket scientist. I asked my usual thousand and one questions. When my inquisition wore them out, I ate my ice cream and went to bed.

Day 5
Tuesday, June 15, 2021

Up early, two packets of instant Quaker Oats with a Larabar. Delicious combo for extreme athletes I think not, but for a biker climbing a 3,000-foot mountain, a proper breakfast. Well, it got the job done.

I had 26 miles to ride with no chance of recharging before I got to Leggett. That was 26 miles away and a 3,000-foot elevation gain. According to Google Maps, the hardest part was at the end, so I needed to conserve my battery as much as possible. Going uphill pulling 65 pounds was going to kill the battery, and I did not want to run out of juice. I kept the battery off downhill and on the flats. Twelve miles of 26 fell into this category. Then uphill. The next 14 miles I went up and up. It did not stop. This is a good thing when touring on a bicycle, as up and down can be maddening.

The ride surprised me—the road, the grade, the trees, the ambiance was exactly like riding up the backside of Mount Tamalpais. I have done that ride hundreds of times, each time swearing, "this is the last time ever." It is not hard, but blind curves with cars whizzing by you is nerve-wracking. This was similar, but add huge redwood logging trucks. I could only imagine what would happen if a truck hit me coming around a turn at 45 mph. Squish is not the right word. I would be a crepe. Crepe de Steve. Leaving at 5:15 am had its advantages; during the first two hours, fifteen cars passed me. Climbing the hill, moving slow is dangerous as the cars coming up on you have little time to react.

Using the battery as little as possible allowed me to use medium power for difficult parts. I made it to the top of the mountain with 28%. I was proud of myself. Climbing a 3,000-foot mountain from sea level pulling a trailer is hard. The last two miles into Leggett were downhill. The next 30 miles were graded downhill. There were still uphill sections, but the hills were neither steep nor treacherous. The town of Leggett was not particularly inspiring; past town near the state campground, I found a spot to eat, read, relax, and recharge my bike for the push into Garberville.

Outside a small town on the way to another small town, I stopped to charge my bike and body at Peg's "Don't Ever Not Stop." Peg's is the real deal. I am glad I stopped. Peg's an anomaly that cannot be explained properly. I bought breakfast and a Monster, proceeded to the patio with stage and picnic tables. A local favorite that sells burgers and smoked oysters. A roadside eatery with hospitality. The first place I met bikers, touring south. They had regular bikes, traveling light by carrying only equipment and food for an afternoon. They were staying at hotels rather than camping. Smart idea.

The day was hot, and I had a few miles in front of me before Garberville. I wanted to travel further, but it was hot, really hot. By the time I left Peg's, the mercury was approaching 100 degrees. I was over the coastal mountains and the heat in the Central Valley was extreme. The bike touring couple told me I was brave riding north. I asked why and got the same response, that the wind would be in my face the whole way, so nobody travels north.

Call me crazy but I never entertained the thought of stopping. I did leave early in the morning and quit in the afternoon to combat the wind. I was at Peg's for three hours charging my bike. I fell asleep at a picnic table and woke hearing my name being called. It was not God calling me but a loudspeaker saying, "Steve, your burger is ready." I almost got up and grabbed his burger, but I am sure he was hungry too. It got crowded while I slept.

I left a tip and thanked them for electricity. My bike was on stage where live music played, so 50 people watched me unplug my bike and mosey on down the road. I wished the smoked oysters a bon voyage and hit Highway 101 with a fresh battery and full stomach.

I rode two hours on roller coaster roads with trucks carrying huge logs. I felt for the trees. I wondered why they were unlucky. It was over 100 degrees. I realized I was dehydrated; I was talking to the dead trees. I rolled past the Garberville sign with 32% of my battery left. I put it on medium power and cruised at 20 mph up the last hill into Garberville.

I took a picture in front of the Garberville sign; I was so dehydrated that the sign was talking to me. I stopped a hundred yards north of the sign at the first motel. It was over 100 degrees; I needed to get out of the heat as soon as possible. I checked into the hotel ($99) and turned on the air conditioner seconds later. I drank two liters of Tang and two pints of water. I took a shower and wandered around the room for 20 minutes talking to the ceiling. If you get seriously dehydrated and start seeing things move that are permanent fixtures, keep drinking water and stay cool. After an hour of drinking water while lying in front of the air conditioner, I came back down to earth.

Garberville is a strange town. I walked through town noticing people were not small town friendly. Not unfriendly but aloof, wary of strangers. I entered a Mexican restaurant and ordered a hamburger with fries. They had nonalcoholic St. Pauli Girl beer. I bought one and told the server she saved my life. She laughed, I smiled. I was back to feeling normal. Normally crazy, but at least the walls were not talking to me.

Day 6
Wednesday, June 16, 2021

I fell asleep at 7:30 pm with the TV and air conditioner blasting. At 4 am, I got out of bed, took a shower, drank two cups of coffee. There is a side road without traffic running through the area. At 4:30 am, there is little traffic on the main road. I rode through town and exited onto Highway 101. Avenue of the Redwoods is a beautiful road, but I did not take it. I stayed on Highway 101.

This morning's ride on Highway 101 through the redwood forest was incredible and bordered magical. It was simply incredible. The long, slow, graceful road was awe inspiring. I turned off the power for an hour because I did not need it. Graceful downhills, no wind, and beautiful scenery. It was perfect. It left an imprint on my mind that I will never forget. I can only describe it as a magical, riding silently down a perfectly smooth highway with no one on it. Truly, the first two hours out of Garberville were magical. Something I would do again.

The miles flew by, and I soon found myself in Del Rio Vista, an old mill town with an operating lumber mill. I rolled in with my battery waning, needing human fuel as well. I stopped at the local EV charging station, but found no hookups for e-bikes, only for Teslas. I cursed Elon for his oversight; this would not be the first or last time I swore at Elon. I was in the middle of a redwood forest with EV hookups for cars, but none for bikes. Everyone says, "it's 110, which is everywhere." Sure, it is everywhere if you live there.

Try riding through a small town and asking people who do not know you for electricity. You look like an alien in a fluorescent green vest riding an e-bike. The first thing you do is ask them for "free" electricity. This does not go over well. Small town friendliness is real, but you need to be careful who you ask and how. Not all small towns are friendly or EV friendly.

Del Rio Vista was friendly. I stopped some locals and chatted for a minute about my plight. I told them I was hungry, asking "Is there a diner nearby?" They said "maybe" which I found an unusual response. They told me about a diner two blocks down the road on the same side of the street. "It is usually closed until 11 am, but it might be open for you." One of the locals pulled out his phone and called the diner. As I approached the closed diner the door opened, and the owner waved me inside.

I met a small group of locals in the closed diner who were sitting around chewing the fat. We conversed about many topics. The proprietor made me a special breakfast of scrambled eggs, bacon, and toast just like my mom would have made. It was excellent, and so was the friendly camaraderie the group extended to me. They gave me advice about the road for the next 50 miles. Part of the road was closed due to a landslide; closed for a couple of hours a day. This information came in handy the next day.

I had a great breakfast, topped off the battery, met great people, and was sad to leave. It was a great experience, a bonhomie feeling, something new generation diners do not have. The meal was prepared with love and kindness, not something you forget.

My next stop was not so fortunate. I experienced the opposite in a town whose motto is "the friendly city": Fortuna, California. I rode into town with high hopes after leaving Del Rio Vista. I saw the city moniker, "the friendly city." I asked where the city park was and went there. I found no place to charge my bike. I asked a local; they could not help me. I asked the park maintenance person, who told me there was no place to charge in the city. The city had blocked public electrical outlets. He apologized for the city being "unfriendly" and pointed me toward the library. He cautioned there was a problem in the past and the city removed all the public places where a person could charge a cell phone. I gave him a look, like "Are you serious?" He apologized again and pointed me to the library.

I received the same response at the library. The town was "friendly" enough to tell me they were "not friendly." The purpose of the "no free electricity" was to thwart "homeless people" from getting too comfortable in Fortuna. The "friendly city" moniker was a farce. I rode out of town on pedal power alone.

Luckily, my ride was flat, as I was now back on the coast. It was not hot, but windy. I rode into the wind through mild hills and came to a desolate marine wildlife sanctuary. The road curved off into the distance. I considered whether to ride two miles into the sanctuary to find electricity or keep pedaling 10 miles into Eureka. I had ridden 62 miles and was getting tired. Riding into the wind feels the same as riding uphill all day. I decided to stop, rest, and look for electricity in the wildlife sanctuary.

I made the right decision. Luck was now back on my side. Life is strange, with one episode of negativity and setbacks followed by one of positive outcomes. I'd just ridden two miles off the beaten path in hopes of finding electricity. I found my outlet, and I found something even more unusual. The park ranger I met had gone to high school in my home county. I passed Drake high school on the first day of my ride. This was unusual to say the least but even more unusual because she had ridden her bike south from Seattle 20 years earlier.

We exchanged stories which had more similarities than differences. The only real difference was the direction we traveled. She rode south, while I was riding north 20 years later. When she left to help another couple, I took a hike around the sanctuary. I hiked for an hour and decided to have a late lunch.

I read for a half hour and fell asleep in the sun. I woke up 45 minutes later. My bike had been charging for three and a half hours. The battery was at 75%. I wanted to ride 18 miles before I broke camp. I said goodbye to Ranger Denise and headed up Highway 101. I conserved the battery as much as possible, as the area was flat. Denise helped map the next 15 miles and told me about a KOA campground.

I rode through Eureka, California, taking the bike path through the outskirts of town. It was pleasant; after having eighteen-wheelers running six inches away for the past two days, it was a nice change. It was heaven for an hour and a half. Then came the most harrowing two miles of my journey.

Good followed by bad was the call of the day. For some strange reason, the City of Eureka built an incredibly scenic bike path and then simply ended it in their old downtown area. Going north to Arcata, you traverse a bridge with zero shoulder for bikers. The speed limit is 55 mph and cars have no patience for bicyclists. I was almost hit by ten cars in a row. It is suicide to attempt this crossing during rush hour. The city engineers should watch their own children cross at rush hour until they get how incredibly dangerous this route is.

I might sound dramatic about this bridge crossing. I am not being dramatic enough. I came inches from death at least four times in less than five minutes. I put my engine into the highest power and rode as fast as I could over the bridge. Cars swerved around me at 65 mph, braking, screeching, yelling, honking, as they tried to run me off the road. It was not an E-ticket ride, but a suicide ride.

If I knew, I would have rented a hotel room and waited until 4 am for an improved chance of a success. It was bad, and once on the bridge, there was no turning back. I live to tell merely by chance, luck, and sheer determination to live. DO NOT ATTEMPT THIS CROSSING! Go around even if it means an extra 10 miles.

After I crossed the bridge of insanity, my heart was racing, and I thought I was going to have a heart attack. Too much adrenaline, not a good thing. I made it to the KOA campground, which is four miles further down the road. The ladies who run the campground were incredibly nice and helpful. I thanked the campground host for her friendly demeanor and pleasant disposition. I was tired and done in. It was as if God put the right person in my path at exactly the right moment. I had ridden 87 miles and felt every single mile. I made dinner—hot dogs, chili, and Mountain Dew—set up my tent, took a shower, and fell asleep with the sun still shining down. It was a long day, a day with many twists and turns. A beautiful day, a terrifying day, and a good night's sleep to come.

Day 7
Thursday, June 17, 2021

I got up early, had breakfast, and was on the road by 5:30 am. My goal was to traverse Arcata on Highway 101 before traffic. With my near-death experiences fresh on my mind, I rode the next 23 miles quickly. I burned up my battery but stopped at a Cal Trans rest area to recharge. I charged in the bathroom for an hour. I chatted with the rest area attendant most of the time.

We lamented; a logging company had purchased the redwood forest behind the rest area. They were logging the area. We could hear one huge redwood tree after another crash down. It was a sickening and heart-wrenching sound; you could feel it as well as hear it. The forest was alive one minute and then deathly silent the next. I contemplated the redwood decks I had built over the years.

Redwood trees are native to Marin County; I grew up with these trees. This was trauma to my soul. It was like cutting off my legs every time I heard the crack and crash of a 100-year-old redwood tree. I know life is about birth, growth, and renewal. These old trees had been logged a hundred years ago and were now being logged again. I realized they could be logged again if we took the time and the energy to replant the forest.

I prayed the logging company had enough sense to replant. I knew my fellow tree huggers would see this through. I posted a video of the destruction. This was the first time I tagged my location posting a video on Facebook, but it was for ecological reasons. My belief is responsible logging and forestry is necessary and, as heart-wrenching as it is, good comes from the rebirth of a forest. Clear-cutting is never pretty, but the tree huggers counterbalance the loggers, and a happy medium is found. Hopefully.

With a heavy heart and half a battery, I left the rest area and headed through a forest of towering redwoods. This area is simply magical. It is like riding through history untouched by humans. The road runs through the old forest saved from the logger's axe hundreds of years ago. I took pictures of huge trees in the magical forest.

There is something special about huge trees. This forest is thousands of years old. It feels mystical; anyone who ventures through it will understand the power behind organisms thousands of years old. Think of the history these trees could tell us if they could talk.

I stopped at an elk preserve. I charged my bike inside the men's room. I spent two hours reading my book and eating lunch, but saw no elk. I communed with nature while I ate. The beauty of everything surrounded me. I did not see elk, but I did see humans taking pictures, walking silently through the park. Small children looked in awe at the trees, with nature surrounding them, which gives me hope that future generations will grow up appreciating the dwindling areas left untouched by man. The elk reserve is one of the beautiful successes where an area has been returned to nature. They used to stage logs and equipment here 75 years ago; now it is a pristine meadow.

This had been an industrial site. When it comes to nature and industry, balance must be found. The money gained from use of an area should be invested into returning it to a natural state. Nature will return, but if man can help as caretakers, all the better. It is balance. Balancing nature and resources can be tough because passions flair and calm minds need to prevail.

Not the easiest thing to accomplish, but worth doing. The elk preserve is a shining example of how man can fix things we've broken. A little forethought can go a long way toward preventing a complete breakdown of ecology. Forethought allows extraction of resources that man needs but still preserves the future. It is about balance of life and nature.

The first 10 miles of the elk reserve were up and down, and the last five miles were down a 1,500-foot mountain pass. It ended at Klamath River, where I stopped at a private campground. I met nice people and enjoyed the rest of the day exploring. I got something to eat at the local diner and relaxed. I rode 61 miles, less than 87 the day before, but enough to make taking the day off rewarding. I was in a good mood even though I suffered my first mechanical failure of the trip. A mechanical failure that would haunt me for the rest of the trip.

The hitch to my trailer broke. I'd bought a special axle for the Burley Bee trailer. The axle stripped and the bolt holding the trailer to the bike detached. I improvised, making do with parts I had. I spent a lot of time and energy making the system work over the next week. Nothing is perfect. Nothing works forever. There was trial and error. Efforts that led nowhere. Solutions became problems in their own making. Forces of nature that countermanded structural integrity. I struggled to make sense of what, where, why, and when of a simple system that failed. Torque, pressure, prolonged tension, and the malleability of metals came into play. I needed a physicist and a mechanical engineer along with a machine shop. I had neither. What I did have was a little ingenuity, determination, and the willingness to learn from my mistakes. I finally devised a system that worked well enough to ride a thousand miles.

I camped in Klamath, California, that night. From the road, you can see the campsite nestled up against the river. It is a huge, privately run campsite. The owners were friendly and helped me patch my bike trailer. They provided a site with an electrical hookup at no extra cost. I ran into people I met at the previous campsite and wondered if they were following me. They were not, but I did tell them my gas mileage was better than theirs.

Day 8
Friday, June 18, 2021

I hit the snooze on my alarm twice; I should not have done so. I needed to pass the rockslide. Part of the road had slid into the ocean; they were fixing it. I slept in for two reasons. One, it was cold; and two, the campsite was on real grass that had been mowed recently. It felt like sleeping on a soft mattress, not solid ground with rocks jutting into you. Sounds funny that one campsite could be so comfortable, but this was like sleeping on a football field. Smooth and level as far as the eye could see. My back loved the campsite. It was warm, soft, cozy, and comfortable in my tent, but I had to go. I was on a mission.

I got out of bed, ate oatmeal and drank black coffee. I broke camp, fiddled with the bike trailer, got the balance right, and off I went. Uphill, more uphill, and then some more uphill. I knew the slide was coming, so I kept the electricity flowing and powered my way up the mountain. I did not know the slide was at the top of the pass. I worried I would miss the 9 am closure. If I did not get past the construction zone before 9, I would wait four hours for it to reopen.

I made it past the construction zone by powering the up-hill ride. I climbed 1,200 feet vertical. There was a flag woman who had me wait a minute; she looked at my bike, then picked up her walkie-talkie. I had a feeling she'd called ahead, telling her counterpart that a bicyclist was coming through and to "expect a delay." She waved the cars through first and then sent me last. It was uphill and I'd just climbed a mountain, but I did not want to make others wait for my slow ass to ride uphill. I put the bike in the highest power and sucked it up.

I caught up to the car ahead of me and powered 25 mph uphill over rough terrain. It was a good incline; I made the quarter mile ride through the construction site as fast as the cars ahead of me. The flag woman looked at me and smiled. She even gave me a thumbs-up. I guess I had impressed her by not dragging my slow ass up and over her construction zone. To be honest, I was fairly impressed with myself. What I did was not easy, so I was breathing hard as I rounded the last turn. I slowed down to drink some Tang and catch my breath. One of the construction workers came over, checked out my bike, and gave me a head bob that said good job. Two minutes later, I was enjoying the fruits of my labor with a long ride down a curvy mountain road.

It was fun and even though I know better, I hit speeds over 35 mph. At one point, I must have been going close to 40 mph. I'd earned it—I had ridden from sea level. It was steep. I flew all the way back to sea level.

I cruised into Crescent City like a victory parade. I was looking for coffee, food, and a place to charge my battery. It was 8:30 am, and the bike shop opened at 11 am. I stopped on the main drag, but did not see a place to charge. My hunger prevailed, so I stopped for a Denver omelet and devoured every morsel. I left shortly thereafter to look for a place to charge my bike.

I went to the city park, where I found electricity in the bandstand. I relaxed in a plastic lawn chair, reading a book while my bike sat charging in Crescent City's bandstand. It looked good up there charging, while I sat security detail. It must have looked unusual because several dog walkers, a guy playing frisbee golf, two local groundskeepers, a businessperson, and a few tourists stopped by to talk to me about my bike. They asked the usual questions. I felt popular and answered questions, including where the restroom was, where beach access was located, etc. I was the park's information kiosk. It reminded me of my mayorship in Elk, California. Everything they asked could be seen from my vantage in the bandstand, so I considered it a public service and repayment to the City of Crescent for the electricity. I even pointed out the free doggy-do bags to enquiring souls.

After a fifteen-minute conversation with a park custodian, he asked where I was going. I explained I was waiting for the bike shop to open. He started laughing, so I asked him, "What is so funny?" Covid had gotten me again. The bike shop had closed three months earlier, a victim of Covid-19 supply chain problems and an inability to pay rent.

The website had not been updated since the shop closed. Not a Yelp or a Facebook posting disclaimed the closure. I rode by the bike shop and saw the boarded-up front door. I said a prayer for those who still suffer the indignity of believing everything they read on the internet and soldiered on. I was still shaking my head two hours later when I stopped to eat lunch. I stopped at a roadside park and used their picnic table to cook chili. If you ever need salt for lunch, try canned chili and Bugles. Tastes great and you will be thirsty for 24 hours.

I took a picture of my next accomplishment. I was now in Oregon. It took a week; I was no longer in California. Another milestone achieved. I celebrated by stopping at the "Welcome to Oregon" sign which is catty-corner to the cannabis store welcoming you to Oregon in a totally different way. I passed on the cannabis and drank a Monster. I like energy drinks, but I did not realize how addictive they were. Tastes great and more caffeine; just what I did not need.

I entered Brookings at 2 pm and went to the local bike shop. It was not much of a shop; what I needed was not in stock. I spoke with the proprietor, who let me borrow a couple of tools to pull my back axle out. I thanked him and left. He steered me to a machine shop that made a replacement hitch. The machine shop was a novelty that had been there for 50 years. The owner knew his business. He manufactured a part out of aluminum which worked but was too rigid; it broke the bike rack two days later. This became a reoccurring phenomenon day in and day out.

I sat writing my notes, then looked outside and saw it was a half hour before sunset. Something inside me said "go see the sunset." The summer solstice was two days away, and it was after 9 pm. I got on my bike and headed north.

Without the trailer and my gear, the bike rode fast and smooth. I found the bike path to Harris Beach State Park. I jetted down a side path through the park and found myself on another path that went to the beach. It was a magical summer night: the wind was still, the fog nonexistent, not a cloud in sight.

The Southern Oregon Coast is rocky with little sandy beaches. It was a picture-perfect evening: the sound of waves, the setting sun, and a scene so beautiful God would be proud. I took a lot of pictures and posted them to Facebook. I shared this moment with 75 people. Some of them locals, but mainly campers from the campground. Everyone felt a sense of magic, so beautiful and inspiring. It made me feel good inside to see couples holding hands and snuggling close to each other. I witnessed children stop playing, hold their parents' hands while we watched the last sliver of sunshine sink into the Pacific Ocean. For anyone who visits Brookings, Oregon, I recommend the beach overlook at the north end of town. You will not be disappointed. If you catch the sunset on a windless night in the middle of summer, you will capture some magic you can pass on to future generations.

There are moments in time a picture cannot capture. It is more than a visual aspect that affects you. It is the energy, the smells, the calm beauty of the moment that is the memory. Those are moments that make life worth living. The moments when the world stops for a second and lets you take it all in. It is times like these that inspire writers and artists. As I left my sunset, I got the hair-raising sensation that runs up your spine. When that happens, you know you've experienced something special. It was that beautiful a night.

Day 9
Saturday, June 19, 2021

I rose early, on the road before 6 am. The coast is flat; conform-ing to the surrounding countryside, it zigs and zags through the area. I saw one beautiful view after another. I stopped to take pictures. A little after 9 am, my battery waning, winds vi-cious, I stopped for breakfast. Fighting headwinds early in the morning is not fun. I had to switch on the battery and pedal into the wind going downhill. The wind tunneling between two hills out of the woods and over a flat stretch of beach made the ride rough.

I normally rest going downhill. I was pedaling hard just to maintain 7 mph. Considering the grade was 4%, I should have been coasting at 15 mph. I was killing the battery I had been conserving over the past hour.

The longer I rode, the better shape I got in; today, I needed the engine to head upwind. I stopped to charge the battery at a coastal park. I plugged in at the bathroom and set up camp at a picnic table. I had brunch: black coffee and oatmeal again. I checked Google Maps, discovering that the next town was still far away. I had ridden 47 miles. I needed food for dinner, but there was nothing around for miles.

I tried to carry enough food and water for a day or two. Carrying large amounts of food over 50 to 60 miles took en-ergy. I took a nap at the picnic table after brunch and read for an hour. When the battery reached 70%, I packed my stuff and hit the road. The wind was still kicking hard, so the next five miles seemed like 50 miles. I had the battery on and was sweating into the wind. The road turned east away from the coast and the next few miles zipped inland.

If you do not believe in dinosaurs, the next part might seem hard to believe. I ran headlong into a T-Rex. I did. I swear I did. I even have pictures to prove it. Ok, it was a replica statue of a dinosaur, but I did run into him. I stopped and took some pictures of T-Rex riding my bike. I'd ridden 10 miles since my last break, but the wind made it feel like 20. I bought refreshments and chatted with the purveyors of the prehistoric park. It was a nice place, so I bought a Rockstar and some chocolate, and off I went. The owner of the T-Rex told me about Humbug State Park, a few miles away. I rode through a forest with a river running through it. I entered the campground and spoke to the rangers. I paid the fee and found a good spot in the hiker/biker area.

The only place to charge my bike was in the bathroom, which was a quarter mile away. I made friends with a couple in an RV site who had two electric bikes. They offered to babysit my bike and let it charge using their electricity. I accepted the offer and was now free to go sightseeing. I headed for the beach.

The beach was at the mouth of a river. A beautiful park, but windy. For entertainment purposes, I watched seagulls soar and drink water from the river. I collected driftwood for a fire and filled my trailer with firewood. I marched back to my campsite and made dinner. I'd planned to buy groceries in town but had ended my ride early, so a baked potato and leftover steak was my only choice, with a box of SweetTarts for dessert. It was still early when a couple of bikers rolled into the campground.

I had been staying in hiker/biker campsites for over a week and had not met another biker. Tonight, I had guests. I welcomed the addition to my solo adventure. I'd passed many bikers with touring gear and wondered where they were staying. There were three other people in camp: a couple and a solo woman rider named Trail. We exchanged stories about our adventures. We headed to the beach and watched the sunset. I enjoyed the company. It was nice meetings others on the trail. Everyone was traveling south. Traveling with the wind rather than against the grain. I was the only one heading north; they agreed I was brave.

I do things backwards. I don't fear going against the grain; if it can be done, I will try it. You may find out why everyone does it that way; other times, you find your way is better, just as good, or novel. Bucking the trend meant riding into the wind, but I had a reason. My reasoning was simple: Alaska is north, so I rode north. Sounded good enough to me, bravery not contemplated.

Looking back, it was a great idea if you have an e-bike. I tell everyone having an e-bike takes wind and hills out of the equation. I find this to be true. Would I tackle the route going north without an e-bike? I do not know but hitting the winds earlier that day made conventional wisdom self-evident. A better question is whether going south with the wind on an e-bike would be a challenge. I plan on trying the southern route on an e-bike to gauge the difference.

Several times, I set up camp then traveled north to pick up supplies. I disconnected the trailer for these trips of two or three miles. When the evening wind picked up, the difference with a tailwind was monumental. You can pedal two or three times and travel a quarter mile; it is that easy.

Heading south on an e-bike with the wind at your back would be easy enough for an amateur. You need riding experience, but training for a 50-mile-per-day ride would be easy. You are still on a bicycle for four to five hours a day. A five-hour ride for the uninitiated is going to be painful. If you ride every day, your butt will not get sore. If you jump on a bike after hitting the StairMaster, you will not have a problem with the physical aspects of the ride, but your ass is going to get sore. My advice is to ride a minimum of 20 miles a day with or without electric just to get your butt into shape for the ride.

Getting saddle sore from riding a bike is real. It is the same pain as riding a horse. To avoid it, ride four or five times a week to get your ass in shape. You could have the strongest legs in the world from running, a StairMaster, tai bo, aerobics, yoga, etc. and still get saddle sore.

I did not suffer saddle sores, as I trained every day for three months prior to leaving. I did a tune-up ride of 300 miles to Yosemite. I was now in central Oregon, and I felt good. I met new friends and ended the night listening to guitar by a campfire. There is nothing better than an evening of good conversation, music, and a campfire. Especially when you have a box of SweetTarts to share.

Day 10
Sunday, June 20, 2021

I left early the next day, after sleeping like a rock. Sunset watching and campfire conversation had worn me out. I'd crashed as my head hit the pillow. I left at 5:30 am, afraid of hitting headwinds again. I rode fast for two hours and reached the outskirts of Bandon before 8 am. There is a highway weigh station outside city limits. I stopped; my battery was 38%. I got on the scale; we weighed 300 pounds. I weigh 164 pounds, and my bike 48 pounds. I unhitched the bike and trailer and found that the trailer weighed 50 pounds. The bike and I weighed 212 pounds. All three were coming out at 300. The math did not add up, so I determined by default that the scale was set to round to the nearest 50 pounds. The trailer must have been 66 to 74 pounds fully loaded with my gear, including the remnants of a box of SweetTarts I'd bought from a dinosaur.

I charged at the Bandon scales for an hour. I drank a Monster and read my book. Re-energized, I rode into the city of Bandon, planning to stop at the bike shop. They did not have the part I needed. What a surprise. I talked to the owner of the store for 20 minutes. He was friendly, knowledgeable about what to expect up the road. It was Sunday morning, so not many people were up at 10 am. I went to a local hot spot diner and used their outlet to continue charging my bike. I did not unplug the open sign but found a double-sided extension cord attached to it. When I told the manager what I'd done, she shrugged her shoulders in acknowledgment of my brazen theft of electricity.

I ate biscuits and gravy with a poached egg. Perfectly caffeinated and re-energized, I mounted my bicycle and headed for Coos Bay. I had 75% when I left Bandon. I enjoyed the first part of my ride, but approaching Coos Bay, I misjudged my battery; it showed 12%. It died on me; I was still eight miles from Coos Bay. That might not sound like a lot, but it was 2, and I'd started at 5:30 am. I was at my limit and still eight miles from my destination. I rode without battery, checking Google Maps to make sure I was not attempting a 500-foot elevation gain. Google Maps lied. I did not hit any major hills, but I did have considerable uphill, albeit a 2.5% grade. Not enough to stop me, but enough to slow me down to 5 mph with a headwind. Hot, sunny, zero shoulder on a busy road. I picked the shortest route into town, not the right one. I do not recommend taking Highway 101 into Coos Bay if you are cycling. There is an alternate route which is longer, but I chose poorly. I missed my turnoff and did not realize until it was too late.

I'd heard about Coos Bay from a Visa commercial years ago; I found the town touristy. Reality hit in when I could not find a place to charge my bike. I had ridden the last eight miles without a battery and my total miles for the day were over 70. I tried a couple of mini malls, the library, tourist traps along the water, the local playground. I got tired and asked Best Western, where I was quoted $225. Too steep for me, especially after spending $10 a day on campsites. I could not stomach the price no matter how tired I was. I went to the city park and looked for hookups, asked locals including kids. They would know where the closest place to charge a phone would be. I kept striking out when I chanced upon a Shakespearean play in the city park. It had large electrical cables stretching to the stage. I asked the stage manager who politely told me sorry but no. She was nice about it but explained that my bike could not be in the play. I understood, so I asked the city pool operator if I could plug in there. I was shot down again; a big sign said, "No Bikes, Skateboards, or Scooters allowed In the Pool Area." Whoops, ok, so now I was out of gas, tired, hungry, and in the middle of Coos Bay, which meant I was lost.

I asked and received helpful hints about where I could find cheaper lodging for the night. I ended up pushing my bike and trailer up the biggest hill in Coos Bay (Google Maps lied to me and told me it was the easiest route). I coasted the next two miles and found a cheap motel, $75 for the night. I was happy; it was in the budget and the lady behind the desk was very helpful.

It was a long day, so I got Chinese takeout food nearby. Before I ate my last wonton, I fell asleep at 7:30 pm. I did not even watch the news; I was out cold. I had ridden 87 miles. I felt like I had ridden hundreds. I slept soundly and woke at 3:30 am. I showered, ate the rest of the Chinese food, and drank motel coffee. I packed my stuff and left on a 100% charge.

Day 11
Monday, June 21, 2021

I left Coos Bay at the break of dawn and rode for two hours. I passed a flat area with a graded highway. I made 42 miles in three hours. It was shortly thereafter that my trailer simply detached itself from my bike and went off on its own adventure. Luckily, like a good dog, it decided to stop and rejoin its master. Out in the middle of the highway, it looked back at me with a grin like, "What are you going to do now?" I was at my wit's end with the trailer and all its manifestations of problems. I put together a simple paper clip and chewing gum solution to get me off the road.

I turned into a campground, which did not have electricity.

I stopped and contemplated my situation, trying to produce a solution to my problem with the parts I had to work with. Seeing my dilemma, a man asked if I needed a hand. I was happy to talk out my problem and see if anyone else had a better solution or idea of how to make this cart work for me. I encountered the right person at the right time. He was a mechanic by trade and a good human being by nature. He took a nut and bolt from his own car and used it to reattach my cart to the frame.

He advised me that the torque on the nut and bolt would eventually wear out and that some device to absorb the tension would be necessary. I agreed with him and explained all the methods I had gone through to get there. I was in central Oregon, exactly 586 miles from home. I'd passed the halfway point in my trip. I was hoping the border would be open and I could travel to Alaska through Canada. I found out later it was not. As I write this a month and a half later, they opened the border yesterday. I celebrated the opening with a silent cheer, looking at pictures of Blaine, Washington, on the news and comparing them to pictures I took a month ago. It was inspiring and felt good to see the exact spot where I had stood and turned back to Bellingham.

I thanked the mechanic from Nevada City, California, and his family who took a personal interest in my trip north. It felt good to have a human help another in need. It lifted my spirits and allowed me to continue my trip north feeling hopeful. It might seem trivial, but this random act of kindness validated my life. When I see someone in need, I help whenever and wherever possible. That is what being a good human is about. We are social beings and helping another without recompense is one of the greatest things a human can do in life. I do it at my own expense and have always done so.

I left with a sense of happiness I had yet to feel on my trip. If the mechanic and his family read this, I thank you from the bottom of my heart for the nut and bolt you offered. Inspired to ride, I continued my way, but I was down to 20%. My battery had conked out at 12% the day before. I needed to charge my battery as soon as possible. I pulled into a campground a few miles down the road. There were no electrical outlets except for one in the camp host's site. I asked the couple occupying the site if I could charge my bike in their site.

They were just poaching the site for a minute while they plotted their next move, not the camp hosts. The electricity to the site was shut off. Bummer. I explained my situation, and they hooked me up to their generator. I chatted with them, sharing stories. Their kids wanted to go rafting and needed air in their raft. We tried to use my bike pump, but it was too small and did not work efficiently. We brainstormed alternatives. We ended up cutting up a plastic Coke bottle and used duct tape to attach it to the exhaust pipe of their vehicle.

Since the truck was cold, it did not melt the plastic Coke bottle and filled the large raft in less than a minute. I cautioned the kids not to breathe in the fumes when they deflated the raft. Like kids, they laughed and promised not to. I wondered if that meant they would do that the first chance they got. At 32%, I decided it was time to hit the road. With seven miles to travel, I wanted to make sure I did not run the battery down. I rode the next seven miles without the battery except on hills.

I turned left into Honeywell Campground before noon. A short-day of riding after yesterday's long day. I found a place to charge my bike and paid for my campsite. There was one person in the campground. I was surprised, as the campground was large and full. I was energized and feeling good. I had interacted with two families I did not know, which made me feel good. It's nice to be around people who mean well, so I went to share my good mood with others.

I set up my tent and went to charge my bike, locking it to a post and praying nothing bad would happen. I wanted to go swimming; I could not be in two spots at the same time. I ended up bike sitting for an hour while eating lunch and reading my book. The call of the lake and desire to go swimming overruled. I disconnected the charger and changed into my bathing suit. I had not swum in a week.

Honeywell Campground is near Dune City, Oregon, appropriately named for the sand dunes prevalent in the area. These dunes are so large, sand surfing or sandboarding is the rage. I wanted to try sand surfing, but did not have time to rent a board in town and get back to the dunes. I settled on swimming in the lake. It was soothing, comforting on my body. After riding for the past two weeks, floating around was enjoyable. I bought a blow-up beach ball for the occasion. I ended up using it many times over the next two weeks. For $2.49, I got my money out of the beach ball.

I watched kids sand boarding, reminiscing on days gone by. I would have been on the slopes one way or another. I still want to try sandboarding; however, I realize I could get injured not knowing the sport and my daredevil ways. I took pictures and vowed if ever in Dune City again, I would try it.

I tried to rent a kayak again. Due to Covid-19, there were no vendors on the lake. Not enough business the previous year; now, the lake was full of people. Nobody was working, so I rode into town, picked up some groceries. They did not have any fresh meat, so I bought hot dogs. It started to rain. I built a fire with damp wood. It did not burn well. I finally got a fire burning and cooked my dogs with a baked potato. I do not like hot dogs, but they are easy to cook when camping by wrapping them in tinfoil and tossing them into the fire.

I ate dinner alone, having plenty to share and thinking a full campground in our area would have latecomers showing up hungry. I was wrong. The guy who was there never stirred. I saw a light on in his tent, but the drizzle was now a steady rain. I called it a night and read in my tent.

I stayed dry and reminisced on my trip so far. I was disappointed that it was raining. It was the summer solstice. The solstices are special days for me. I wanted to watch the sunset over the ocean on the longest day of the year. The modern world seems to forget the meaning of solstices. The longest and the shortest days of the year are celestial events, larger than humankind and something man has relied on for hundreds of thousands of years. They mark the beginning and the end. A celestial event should not be forgotten.

I view the solstices like New Year's. They mark not just a change of seasons, but time gone by. Most people have New Year's resolutions. I quit those when I was in my twenties. I started my own New Year's tradition; every January 1st I do something I have never done before. Whether it is going to a different restaurant, playing golf at a new course, or mountain biking someplace new. It does not have to be anything special, just something I have never done before, or a place I have never been.

It is a lot easier to do this than make New Year's resolutions. It is also something you can do if you are in a relationship or have a family. There is something gained by doing something new. I call these good things. Good things are worth doing. Leave January 1st for recovering from the night before. Make your life changes on the solstices. Try it; you will like it.

One thought went through my mind. The same thought was reinforced in every town I passed, every store, restaurant, shop, or business. Every one of them had a "help wanted" sign. I took a month off to make the trip, but my job was just "a job." It was not a career, just a place to make pocket money while writing stories and reading my books. I thought, "Why am I so attached to the city?" It was home for most of my life, but I'd lived in many places, including Los Angeles, Santa Barbara, and Marin County. Most of my life was spent within a ten-mile radius of my current apartment. I was not particularly happy with my place or my job. Why stay?

The thought of starting over somewhere else started in Marin County. By the time I left Sonoma, I had seen enough "help wanted" signs to plant a seed in my mind. The thought of making this a one-way trip started as a concept. The concept grew to an idea, which motivated me to action. As I read in my tent that night, the rain pitter-pattering outside, I realized this was not another adventure. I was looking for a new place to live, a whole new life. A whole new everything. I did not make this decision lightly. I was leaving everything behind: friends, family, job, apartment, financial security. I thought it through for two weeks and knew I was about to step off a cliff. This realization helped me decide my future. I knew I was not going back, but where would I live. Alaska?

This ends the first half of my ride. The second half takes a different tone. I have no intention of returning to San Francisco. I knew then I was not going back. The decision was made. I fell asleep with my head in a book, which is common. It happens often. I slept with my mind at ease, looking forward to the future from a new vantage. The summer solstice marked the change.

Day 12
Tuesday, June 22, 2021

It was soggy and drizzling when I got up. I ate breakfast: leftover hot dogs and instant oatmeal. I had a couple cups of coffee and hit the road. I stopped three times to charge my bike. I ran fast through the morning and was down to 32%, so I pulled into a semiprivate campground on the Oregon coast. I plugged into an outlet in the bathroom and crossed a footbridge to eat lunch at a picnic table. I read for an hour and got back on my bike two hours later. I rode through a coastal area that parallels the beach. The wind picked up early, and I found myself tiring.

I pulled into town and stopped for coffee in Yachats, a little town with a mountain village feel to it. I met a couple e-bikers touring south. They told me about a campground outside Newport called South Beach. They were a few years older than I; their destination was San Diego. They had nice e-bikes, and

I envied their battery capacity. They had modified the original battery capacity, which was double mine. They were traveling with light panniers on the front and back. It did not look like they had camping gear; they had done this before and had what they needed.

They were traveling 50 to 60 miles a day. With their battery capacity, they did not have to stop and recharge. I was envious. We talked while my battery was charging at the coffee shop. I ended up watching their bikes for them while they went to the store. We said our goodbyes, I finished my coffee, and off I went down the road.

I stopped at a Mexican restaurant near Waldport and ate lunch at a patio table while charging my bike. I had a bridge to cross in Waldport. I'd learned to rest and charge before attempting bridge crossings. With a full belly and a fresh battery, I stormed the bridge, which was easier than I thought. I was feeling pretty good about my ride, but later in the afternoon the wind picked up significantly. I was running out of juice and had misjudged my destination by a couple of miles. It was painful; the road followed the contours of the land, and I found myself completely out of juice about four miles from South Beach. I decided to grit it out without a battery.

I made it, of course, but once you ride 57 miles, you do not want the last four uphill into the wind. I was happy to turn into the park, which lived up to its expectations. There was an electrical hookup in my campsite. Cost $10. I refreshed with Gatorade and ice cream. Nothing better than ice cream to cheer me up and re-energize. I was the first biker in the hiker/biker area, but not the last by any means. By sunset, there were eight of us. I really enjoyed the camaraderie and company. I was alone most of my journey and had expected to meet more people touring. I was a novelty amongst my peers. I was the only one crazy enough to head north. I was glad to have my e-bike at this point; some of the hills I had crossed that day would have been extremely difficult if I did not have help. My nemesis, bridges, became a nuisance but not a death trap.

I went into town and bought precooked ribs. I started a fire and cooked them, allowing the other hiker/bikers to use my fire. I encouraged everyone to share, and we had a good time. I was encouraged by another girl who was riding to San Francisco from Washington state. I was impressed with anyone doing this alone, especially women. She was not the only single girl I would meet along the way. I enjoyed the conversation with all the hiker/bikers, but especially women daring to make the journey solo.

I spent time riding around the campground that evening. It was full, packed to capacity. After Covid-19, it was nice to see people getting out and about again. I went to bed early that night. I was wiped out from a long day. I listened to the voices of other riders around the campfire as I drifted off to sleep.

Day 13
Wednesday, June 23, 2021

I left South Beach at 6 am, hitting the snooze bar twice. I ate my usual breakfast: oatmeal and black coffee. I love riding early in the morning. I left with a full battery, planning to stop at the North Face outlet in Lincoln City, Oregon. I needed new rain gear. I had a couple hours before the North Face store opened, so I left the battery on full power and flew down the highway at 24 mph. I was burning up the battery but did not care. I was enjoying a full power cruise. On full power, the bike does 28 mph, even pulling a cart, but heading into the wind, you will only get 25 miles out of the battery. You do not have to work hard; the miles are a lot of fun.

I traveled 27 miles to Lincoln City in an hour and a half. I went to McDonald's and got a big breakfast. The two packets of oatmeal and coffee were not enough fuel. I headed up the road to the North Face store, which opened at 11 am. I scouted a place to charge my battery and came up empty-handed. I circled the outlet mall and saw several possibilities, but when I plugged my charger in, I found no juice in the outlet. I was despondent; there was a Tesla charging station in the parking lot, but no e-bike station. I found my answer next to the picnic table. I reached behind the Coke machine and unplugged it. Then I plugged in my charger; problem solved.

I sat by the now dead Coke machine, praying nobody came to use it so I could charge my bike. The maintenance crew said hello and nothing about my bike, which they clearly saw. At 10:30 am, the security guard came on duty, walked by. I said hello, we exchanged pleasantries. I sat charging my bike, and the poor Coca-Colas were getting warm. I drafted a letter to Elon pleading if Tesla helped us poor e-bikers, the people of Lincoln, Oregon, would not have warm Coke. I posted it on an obscure website dedicated to EVs. I wonder if he read it. It merely explained the connection between e-bikes and warm Coca-Cola.

At 11 am, the North Face outlet shop opened. I was the first one in the store. The manager directed me to rain gear, and it took me three minutes to pick out what I wanted. I got a jacket and matching pants, last year's model. I walked out for less than $100. I got a good deal, which made me happy. I was ready to head out in any weather.

I found a bike shop in Lincoln City, but it was closed. My luck with bike shops was not good. I had 60% on my bike and wanted to make Pacific City before day's end. That was 23 miles away. I rode casually until I came to a big hill. I did not plan my battery usage well, so by the time I traversed the twelve-mile hill, I had 12%. Large hills were draining my battery quickly. I had eight miles left, which isn't much, but when you are going up steep hills pulling a 65-pound trailer, eight miles can seem like an eternity. I started looking for places to top off my battery. I came upon a retirement community RV park. It was an exclusive club, a gated compound. I rode up to the kiosk and saw an electrical outlet. I plugged in and ate lunch on their lawn. Sliced cheese and salami on Ritz crackers. I washed it down with a green Monster. I'd started relying on Monsters. I noted they were not keeping me up at night. I was burning off the calories and the caffeine as fast as my bike was burning the battery. They make me happy, so I made no attempt to stop drinking them.

My caffeine intake had tripled. I drank a cup of coffee a day before my trip. Caffeine had no visible effect now. Exercise and camping burn calories. My calorie intake had skyrocketed; many calories were coming from Monsters and Rockstars.

An hour later, my picnic over, I decamped from the exclusive RV grounds and headed down the road to Pacific City. I used the battery sparingly over the next eight miles. It was downhill, then flat. I rolled into Pacific City before two o'clock and found the county campground. They told me it was full; under county Covid guidelines, not state. I looked around; they had five campsites full out of twenty.

I was tired from riding 50-plus miles, and my battery was dead. They made a phone call and received an exception for me. I was going to be there one night. Good karma came through. I ended up paying $25 for a campsite with an electrical hookup. That is a good deal along the Pacific Coast. I set up my tent quickly; it was 2 pm, a beautiful day, and the area looked favorable for a walk into town. I left my bike charging in good company. I occupied the site next to the host, and they promised to keep an eye on it. The chance of someone stealing my bike was low, as the area was quiet. If anyone did, they would be noticed.

I walked into town and saw a kayak rental. It was right on the river. I knocked on the door and saw 20-plus kayaks on the dock. I wanted to paddle around for an hour or two. Nobody answered my knock. I looked around; a sign said, "Closed on Wednesdays." Just my luck, today was Wednesday. Oh well,

I went to the store and purchased a Monster and Bugles. I went to the city park, ate Bugles, fed the birds. They must have been well-fed, as they were not interested in my Bugles. The squirrels liked them. I continued into town and went to the hardware store.

Shopping in little towns, especially hardware stores, is always fun. Most hardware stores do not do much business with tourists; they deal with locals. If you ever want advice, go to the local hardware store. There is always some guy that has worked there since time began and will know everything. He will know more about the town than anyone else. At some point, all the locals go to the hardware store. They buy what they need to fix a problem. They know everyone in town and what they do. The hardware store is in the center of town, looks like it has been there since when the town began. Pacific City could have started because of the hardware store.

I told the guys about my cart breakdowns. They recommended a hitch that mountain climbers use for rock climbing. It was rated 1,500 pounds. It looked like it might work, so I bought two of them, different sizes. One worked so well it stressed the cart in another area, which broke the hinge on the trailer arm. There was not enough play in the part to allow the cart to sway. The hinge holding the arm to the cart had a catastrophic failure. Aluminum parts fail when there is inordinate stress for an extended period.

I now use the hitch as a key chain. My ten keys do not give it much of a challenge. It worked; just too well. C'est la vie. After I had made my $10 purchase, I continued through town and crossed the river. I watched a fisherman casting. He caught a large salmon but threw it back. He was fishing for the sake of fishing.

I was impressed with his catch. I was even more impressed when he threw it back. I continued walking to the beach. I saw a sign advertising camel rides. I did not see any camels, but the sign looked legit. There was a corral with a high fence. I kept looking for camel tracks but found none. No kayak, no camels. At least I got to see salmon.

I talked to a couple of tourists in town. They lived 50 miles inland and had come to beat the heat. Pacific Beach has a nice beach, a quarter-mile wide. There is a large sign saying, "ok to drive on the beach" if you go left, but an even larger sign on the right saying, "no cars past this point." Going left was ok but not right. I could not see a difference between the two. I am sure there is a reason for the rules.

I traveled two miles on foot, then I turned back and headed home. Home being my campsite. I stopped at the grocery store to pick up supplies for a couple of days. They looked at me funny because I had just been there. I did not want to be weighed down with supplies on my walk. I went back to camp, cooked a steak, baked a potato, and called it a night.

Day 14
Thursday, June 24, 2021

The bike was fully charged in the morning. I rode back the way I came through town. I took the scenic route near the ocean. I rode the first 30 miles in less than two hours using 70% of the battery. I had fun riding fast. I pulled into a private campsite and bribed the owner into letting me use their electricity for two hours. I made a second breakfast at a picnic table and read for two hours. I talked to a few locals who were living in the RV park. There are two different rates charged at RV parks: one for long-term residents and another for those "passing through." Every RV park had the same policy. I wondered how many people live like this across America. If you get tired of one place, move to another. Most people were retirement age. There are many adventurists—the discoverers, the explorers of the world. I belong to the explorers, always wanting to see what else is out there.

I love exploring new places, doing new things. If there is a place I have not seen, I want to go. Given the opportunity, I would travel the world and write stories. That is my life. I want to see everything, do everything. There is nothing wrong with this approach. The reason for my journey was to explore an area of the world I had never seen. To see my fiftieth state. If I had time and money, I would add countries to my bucket list, not states.

Not everyone has the itch to explore; others have it bad. People ask, "Where are you going and why?" I tell them "Alaska" and "Because I have never been before, a good enough reason for me." Going on an adventure takes less planning rather than more. If you want to see things in life, you can't make rigid plans. You must allow time to wander off the beaten path and explore side roads. I have never been down this road before, so every road is a side road. Meeting people along the way and hearing their stories is part of the journey.

It is said, "You can live a thousand lives by reading books." I am an avid reader; I have lived a thousand lives and more. If I add all the *Time*, *Life*, and *National Geographic* magazines I've read, maybe two thousand lives. You can read a lot in 50 years.

Hearing other people's stories is like reading a book. People have incredible lives and have done great things. Others have adventures exploring far-off places. Listen to them and live vicariously through their stories. I share my stories and adventures; stories so outlandish people think I am fabricating. They get to know me and realize I am telling the truth. There are many paths in life; you decide which ones to take. Some of these paths are fraught with danger and peril. Many paths I do not recommend, but someone needs to take them to tell others. My life story is filled with stories I would rather not repeat. I do not mean I won't tell them to others, but I do not want to repeat them.

I am more cautious these days but still love an adventure. I do things more carefully now. Plan for the worst, hope for the best. I still make wrong turns and live with the consequences, but I think things through before I do them. It was not always that way. If something sounded good, I tried it and damned the consequences. I lost a lot of blood and money doing crazy things. You get wiser with age, which is a good thing, and healthier.

I left the RV park and rode for another hour and a half. I was in Tillamook, Oregon. I am a big fan of cheese; I passed the Tillamook Cheese factory with a conflicted heart. I wanted to stop and take the tour, but I have been on factory tours before, and I can watch it on YouTube. I know how to make cheese, what it is made from. I said "thank you" to the cows I passed for 50 miles. I knew they were helping Tillamook make cheese. I thanked them again as I passed later that day. The cows munched on grass and looked with a curious glance as I rode past.

I stopped at Denny's in Tillamook. I wanted a Grand Slam. I was long overdue for a Slam. I looked for a place to charge while eating but did not see an outlet. I did see an open table right next to the window. I could watch my bike and eat my Grand Slam. I am glad I did for two reasons. One, I enjoyed my brunch thoroughly. The second was I met Jeff. Jeff is an e-bike enthusiast. He told me about his e-bikes and methods improving them. He has YouTube videos demonstrating multiple batteries and motors on his e-bikes. He had pictures of his bikes and demonstrated the solar panel system he used in remote places. We also discussed different battery voltages and the problem with different types of batteries and engines to run e-bikes.

I could discuss a lot of technical problems and solutions regarding e-bikes. There are many misconceptions about e-bikes, power methods, watts, battery size, recharging, etc. I leave this to the third part of my book. The technical details are just that, technical. I do not want to bore you to death. If you are looking for technical information, skip to the third part of my book.

I am glad I met Jeff; we spent an hour talking outside Denny's in Tillamook. He gave me new ideas and different avenues of building something better down the line. My bike left a lot to be desired for touring. The Vado was built for getting around town quickly rather than touring over long distances. Rather than modify the bike, I modified my plans and stopped to recharge often. A tortoise and hare story. My bike is quick like a rabbit, but has a small battery. I went fast for a few hours, then became a tortoise, reading books, charging the battery.

An exercise in frustration, most of the time, but it allowed me to rest, relax, and gain perspective on what I was doing. I stopped to breathe, take in the scenery, and write about my trip. What I did on my ride was just as important as riding, which brings up an unexpected benefit of the two-hour delay talking to Jeff: I ended my ride eight miles from my intended destination.

The wind picked up as I traversed a canyon. The wind became a tunnel off the sea. I had 32% when I passed a private campground, Kelly's Landing on Nehalem Bay. I rode past it at 18 mph and started to round the bend, then I just stopped. I stopped for no reason and turned around. They were advertising it as a Crab Shack campground, and anyone who knows me knows I love crab. Crabbing is great fun; I wanted to catch them.

I entered Kelly's Landing, one of the better decisions on my trip. They had a campsite with electricity. They charged me $35 for the night. This was the best $35 I spent on my trip. I set up camp between two large fifth-wheels; I was happy to have a slice of heaven. My spot looked out on the docks, where 50 people were crabbing with rented equipment. They were catching crabs; a couple had a whole bucket full of them. I was content to watch. Had it been earlier in the day, I would have rented equipment for the day. I settled for having a crab dinner. I made a complete mess of myself. Eating crabs with your fingers is messy. I loved it, took pictures, and went back to my campsite stuffed and happy. I made coffee and read for a few hours. The place offered showers, so I took a long one. The shower took quarters, and I had a bag full of them. I felt great, clean, and shiny. I turned my lantern on and read for a couple hours before calling it a night.

It was calm on the bay; the sunset was beautiful—the best I had seen since Brookings. The days were passing quickly. I was enjoying my adventure and had a great day. I only rode 47 miles; I'd planned more, but I was happy. I bought some chocolate at the crab shack and went to sleep shortly after sunset, eating Hershey's and Junior Mints. I was happy.

Day 15
Friday, June 25, 2021

I woke at 4:30 am and got back on the road by 5:30 am. My journey today had a finite destination, Fort Stevens at the mouth of the Columbia River. I had been warned about the Astoria-Megler Bridge many times. I intended to cross it early Saturday morning when traffic would be at a minimum. My intention was to cross as quickly as possible using as much electricity as required to do so. Fort Stevens is the closest campground to the bridge. I could stay in a hotel in Astoria, but I chose Fort Stevens. They named it after me, so I figured I best check it out.

I had a mountain to climb this morning. I knew it and worked hard to minimize my battery use. I wish Mission Control (the navigation system built by Specialized) had an altimeter. I never knew how high I was and how much farther I was from the top. Google Maps is not good at this either. My inclination and declination totals were accurate, but it could not tell when I reached the zenith. It also worked only when I had an internet connection. Road maps make everything look flat; they give you a false sense of reality. Hills and mountains are obstacles that bicycle riders need to be aware of. Not knowing how high or how much more you need to climb your obstacles can have negative consequences.

I would invest in technology that allows your phone to plug into your bike's battery. My bike's battery is larger than my iPhone battery. Specialized Mission Control uses your iPhone battery quickly. Even with it fully charged, riding through mountainous terrain, where a signal is difficult, turns the power up on the battery. This drains a fully charged iPhone in three to four hours. When you are in the middle of nowhere, it is nice to navigate without draining your phone.

I turned off Mission Control. Google Maps does the same thing, turns up the power use on your phone. When I was out in the middle of nowhere, I had no navigation system or phone. If Mission Control and Google Maps were on, you could see the battery drain in real-time. It was a problem. I solved it by turning off my phone. I turned it back on when I went through town.

I was going up a big hill. My muscles told me, my lungs told me. Just when I thought I should take a break, my trailer unhitched. I made an impromptu adjustment, and off I went again, but now it was downhill. During the next few miles, I hit speeds above 35 mph. I topped out at just under 42 mph. I do not suggest this for any bike rider; whether e-bike, racing bike, or any bike, it is not safe to go that fast. Bicycles are not designed for that speed. Pulling a bicycle trailer—especially one that has disconnection problems—that fast is not advisable, and after a few minutes of reckless abandon, I slowed down to a balmy 25 mph. Soon enough, my hill gave way to a short uphill and then flattened out completely.

Long live the daredevil in me; it is fun to go flying down big hills, but please do so with caution and your mental acuity in good working order. Having done this before, I know what happens when a blowout or a brake failure occurs. At high speeds, the amount of stress on bike parts intensifies quickly and you need to be prepared for anything. You also need to know how to crash effectively, how to lay your bike down at high speeds. Any person that has ridden motorcycles will tell you this can save your life. Not knowing how to do this can kill you quickly. Knowing how does not provide protection from great bodily harm. It lessens the likelihood of death and dismemberment, but the key word here is "lessen the likelihood" and not prevent the likelihood.

Some humans thrive on the danger. It is an adrenaline rush for sure. Some of us have a predilection for adrenaline. The term adrenaline junkie is real. The adrenaline release from doing dangerous things can be addicting. I caution all riders about the effect of such. I suffer from "adrenaline junkie" effect. I love it; it makes you feel alive. A sensation sought after by skydivers, rock climbers, and cliff divers. There are hundreds of sports and activities catering to adrenaline junkies. I would do them all given time and opportunity, but I am now at a point when I need to balance these activities with the realities of age.

I have no intention of quitting the lifestyle. I do not think I can. Will it kill me? I doubt it. I am old enough to know better and believe I make better decisions and quantify the cost-benefit principle. Meaning, I know the fun and benefits of adrenaline-seeking activities but also the cost of doing so. My days of rock climbing and cliff diving are over. My body cannot deliver against mistakes. Bones get brittle, cartilage not so spongy. Things break and snap easier as you age. Will I give up downhill on my bike? No. Why? Because I balance my speed accordingly. I still get the adrenaline rush, but at a slower speed. I have crashed enough times in my life to know what happens when you do. It is not fun, and the older you get, the longer it takes to recover. I do things that seem crazy, but the condition of my body plays a significant role in the decision. I make mistakes, but my mistakes are few and far between. Call it adrenaline wisdom. Like everything in life, find balance in what you want and reality.

My daredevil excursion over, heart racing, I slowed down and found a new rhythm for the next 20 miles. This portion of my ride consisted of long, slow uphill and downhill sections of graded highway. The shoulder was negligible, the thought of being hit by a logging truck never far from my mind. That did not give me an adrenaline rush; it kept my mind attuned, aware of my surroundings.

Even a short day's ride can leave you mentally drained without realizing it. Spending a few hours with your mental radar on high alert for danger can wear you down. Riding long distance over a period of weeks affects not just your arms, legs, and back; it affects sight, sound, and mental acuity. Do not underestimate mental exertion from a long day of riding. You must remain vigilant, always aware of what is in front of you. Sudden obstacles, potholes, tree branches, animals, etc. can appear at any time. If you veer from the shoulder to avoid an object, there might be cars in the lane next to you. You must know your stopping distance and brace yourself for obstacles. This is replayed every second you ride, and it gets tiring.

A single mistake, even at low speeds, can cause death. A car or truck hitting a bicyclist is not a good thing. If this happens, you are going to have a bad day. You will be lucky to survive with broken bones. Many people die because they aren't aware of their surroundings, and they veer into traffic. Electric cars are silent when approaching from behind. Do not wear headphones. Listening to music on a speaker at low volume is ok. Do not drown out road noise.

Another danger of traveling at a high speed: wind creates its own noise. Traveling 35 mph on a bike creates 35 mph wind speed. Great care should be given to the wind effect when traveling at high speed. You will not hear cars coming. Always ride defensively when on the road.

After 35 miles, I pulled into a RV campground, bribing the owner $5 to charge in the back of their store. I bought a blueberry muffin and coffee, set myself in the shade behind the store.

I read my book, ate a muffin, and drank coffee at a bench out back. While multitasking, I met a lady named Jenny who was doing her laundry.

Jenny is a schoolteacher from Chattanooga, Tennessee. We chatted for an hour. We talked about everything under the sun. I was impressed with the schoolteacher from Tennessee; she'd driven her Subaru teardrop trailer across the country. She did it for an adventure and a story. We traded stories about where we had been, what we had seen. We talked about places all over our country. We were on different paths but shared the same passion. The passion to explore. To see new places, new things, and have experiences we could share with others. She does so directly in her classroom. My plan is to write about them. Experiences worth writing about are everywhere, so go out and do them. Quit talking about it. Just do it.

The end goal: you can live a thousand lives from stories I pass on. When you meet someone, it opens a whole world of ideas. There is a direct connection to wisdom by talking and communicating with other humans. You gain wisdom over the years and pass it on. This is what makes humanity incredible. Your story has a special wisdom that only you can pass on to others. The internet is a great example of collective wisdom, but it is not the only source. Talking and writing benefits society, adds your collective wisdom to the data pool. Writing this book is an example of using collective wisdom to help future generations.

I left the roadside RV park knowing I'd met someone special. Our chat—albeit only an hour—will affect hundreds of others down the road. Jenny's story touched me in a good way; I am sure mine had the same effect. Part of our conversation will end up in the hearts and minds of her students. That is one example of how humans interconnect one human at a time. You cannot get this by surfing the internet.

I rode into Fort Stevens an hour and a half later, 46 miles in total. I was done. I paid for my campsite and was the first in the site. It was a beautiful site with an electrical hookup. The State of Oregon went above and beyond the call of duty helping bikers traverse their great state. The campgrounds and services are excellent in their parks. They are a shining example of what we should do with State Parks for the future. Recreational space is essential to maintain humanity as we know it.

I set up my tent and charged my bike while cooking left-overs, multitasking. I went on a ride traversing Fort Stevens, which sits at the mouth of the Columbia River near Astoria, Oregon. The Park reminds me of the Presidio in San Francisco. The similarities include gun batteries and tunnels connecting them. It is beautiful with beach access and views of the bridge. I had a five-mile-long bridge to cross the next morning. Not much different than the Golden Gate, not as high but longer. I put the notion aside. It was a hot day, so I went to find ice cream, Ben and Jerry's Cherry Garcia.

I love ice cream and books. Combine the two, and I am in heaven. I went to the beach and read with my ice cream dripping on my beach towel. I washed myself off in the lake, then read in the lake using my styrene mattress as my floaty. I conversed with locals; they had paddleboards. I vowed the next chance I got, I would rent a kayak or paddleboard. Luck and Covid-19 worked against me. My beach ball and foam mattress would have to suffice for the time being.

I finished my ice cream and headed back to camp. I stopped to gather firewood and was glad later that night. The mosquitoes were fierce. My campfire provided little protection; it also brought me a few visitors. I met people that night. One guy with a solar-paneled e-bike who rode from Portland to escape the heat. A girl was riding to San Diego. I am impressed with women who tour solo; maybe they are my kindred spirits, doing so many things alone. I can never find anyone crazy enough to accompany me.

Day 16
Saturday, June 26, 2021

Up early drinking coffee, eating oatmeal at 4:30 am. I had a bridge to cross; I was not looking forward to it. I was looking forward to entering Washington State. Oregon was good to me, but I was ready for the next phase of my journey.

Bridges are my nemesis; they are not fun. You have no shoulder and cars own the road. This was a long bridge. From one entrance to the other was five miles. The on-ramp from the Aberdeen side is a mile long and goes up a steep incline for a quarter mile. I had been mentally preparing myself for the challenge for a half hour. When the on-ramp finally loomed before me like a roller coaster, I did not hesitate. It was Saturday morning, 6 am, there was an onshore breeze. I had warmed up; I'd done my stretching and was ready. I put my e-bike into the highest power. This was not a hill but the beginning of a gauntlet for a biker pulling a trailer. I wanted to get this over with.

In the e-bike's highest power setting on flat terrain, hitting a speed of 28 mph is possible. If you have a tailwind or a slight downhill grade, you can easily hit speeds of 30 to 32 mph. Pulling a bike trailer with 65 pounds of gear makes it a little more difficult, but still doable. At the bottom of the bridge, my battery registered 84%. I charged the hill, taking me to the highest point on the bridge using leg muscles and engine. By the time I got to the pinnacle, my legs and lungs were burning. I pushed harder. One car passed me, and then I was over the top; I had a long declination on my horizon. I pedaled harder. My speedometer showed 31 mph. I kept pushing and continued to the portion that flattens out. I kept the battery in the highest power and pushed my body, mind, and soul to ride like the wind. Two more cars passed me and then a large truck. My bicycle shuddered with the truck buffeting me closer to the railing. I was doing 26 mph, pulling a trailer that swayed with every car and truck that passed me. The cars were passing me at 60 mph with three inches to spare. Not my idea of fun.

I kept my courage, wits, and speed up as I entered a long, semi-flat stretch for two miles. I pumped my legs and body like a mad man trying to win a race. Two more cars passed me during the next eight minutes and soon I was approaching my last hurdle. Another hill of medium size, it allows boats to pass under the bridge. My lungs burned with exhaustion; I pumped my legs as hard as I could. I went up and over the last portion as three more cars and a truck passed me. One car honked, giving me a fist pump to encourage me on. He had a Thule bike rack on top of his Subaru; I felt his empathy from a hundred yards. I reached the top of the bridge and had a quarter mile downhill. I pushed all the way to the end as hard as I could.

I conquered my nemesis; my bridge was crossed. Twelve cars and trucks had passed me on the crossing. I exaggerate my fear of bridges only slightly. I took this crossing as a challenge, and I conquered it. I stopped shortly after crossing, taking in the scenic overview next to the "Welcome to Washington State" sign. I took pictures. The whole crossing took less than fifteen minutes, five miles. I was elated and physically exhausted from the sprint. The endorphin release was real; I sat there for 10 minutes enjoying the view and taking more pictures. I posted them to Facebook. My feat was nothing in the grand scheme of things, but to me it was another milestone. I was now in another state, and I had crossed a bridge that was both proverbial and real.

I stopped a few hundred yards from the bridge, as my cart was acting funny. I rode over a curb into the rest area. My trailer started scraping the ground. I looked back, realized something was wrong. Really wrong. I pulled over to investigate the latest problem with the trailer. I was lucky this did not happen on the bridge. I would have been turned into a speed bump—roadkill de Steve. The aluminum bracket holding the arm of the trailer had suffered a catastrophic failure. It had snapped in two. The only thing holding the arm to the trailer frame was some nylon fabric that had caught and wrapped around the now broken bracket.

It took me 45 minutes to strip the bracket off the other side of the cart and remount it. A good thing they made the cart reversible. You can switch sides for mounting, which gave me two spare brackets in case of failures. The stress was too much and the curb I rode over snapped the bracket in two. So much for aluminum and catastrophic failures. I remounted the extra bracket. I was back up and running shortly thereafter. I had a choice: go left or right. Going left was longer but avoided a 1,000-foot incline over the next 36 miles. The other way you got the hill and subtracted 10 miles. I could have flipped a coin, but I decided to go the shorter, steeper route more on a whim than anything else. Ten extra miles over a thousand-mile ride did not concern me. Far from it. The way I chose went through two small towns and I wanted to charge my bike in one of the towns.

I went right, inland. The first 12 miles of my ride used 48% of the battery. That is a lot, but running the bridge at full speed took its toll. I made for Nashelle, Washington. I arrived with 32% battery. I found a convenience store with an ice machine out front. I saw an electrical socket next to it and plugged in my bike. It was 8:30 am and the store opened at 9. Next to the store was a little league field with two teams practicing.

The kids were in uniforms, looking sharp and alive. I sat in the shade, eating a power bar, drinking Tang. For the next half hour, I watched them practice. Then at 9 am, the game started. I watched the game and realized I was enjoying this more than an MLB game. I love baseball; I played little league. I was deep into memories of years gone by. I sat reminiscing about games I played, starting with T-ball. I love the sport, so watching the kids play was heaven. I was not rooting for a team; I just enjoyed the game.

It was 9:45 am when I left the game and went to find my bike. I entered the store and apologized for stealing their electricity. My confession was met with a smile, as the lady behind the counter said, "No problem, any time you want you can charge your bike here." I was happy and thanked her several times. I quizzed her about the road ahead. I wanted to know what to expect. She said, "Bring water—it is going to get hot as you go inland." I listened; I bought two more Gatorades, one liter of water, and two Monsters. I exited the store. With 58%, off I went.

The next 25 miles were pleasant. I alternated between the battery and switching it off when it was flat or a declination. I wound through canyons that had been logged extensively. A quarter mile clear-cut and then a quarter mile left intact. I got used to the devastation and realized the clear-cut areas were alive with regrowth, plenty of wildlife, and berries growing. The birds and bees had moved in and were thriving. It was healthy land—for birds, bees, and bears. I passed a few elk, deer, and cows that stared.

It was hot as I traveled inland. I entered a forest and craved the shade. There was a heat wave in the area; they claimed the worst ever. It was 110 degrees in Seattle. It was hotter where I was. Everybody was talking about it. I rode 50 miles; the thermometer was 108 degrees. I pulled into Bruceport County Campground. I spoke with the lady who ran the campground; she let me charge my bike at the host site. Some sites had electrical hookups and were designated for RVs. They had no sites available with electricity, but my hiker/biker site was convenient, and in the shade. I bought firewood and made camp. With my bike charging at the host site, I was now free to explore the area on foot. There was a trail to the beach of a large bay. I went down to the shore and scouted around. It was desolate and muddy. Not someplace you want to go swimming. I hiked back up the trail and came across an area covered with berries. They were black-, red-, and salmon-colored berries.

I was not sure if they were edible. I picked a few and hoped I could get an internet connection to research my berries.

I stumbled across the husband of the camp host; I asked him about my berries. He told me some were black berries; the others were salmon berries. They were both edible. He showed me wild berries which are really blueberries, but not the type you buy in the store. They tasted good. With my new-found berry education, I went berry picking. I had a good time and soon had plenty of berries for dessert. I went back to my campsite and cooked a steak with a baked potato. I had fresh berries and cream for dessert. I sat for two hours and watched the sunset from my campsite reading a book. It was peaceful, and very quiet compared to the last two campgrounds.

Day 17
Sunday, June 27, 2021

I got up early, hit the snooze on my phone. I slept until 5:30 am, then ate leftover steak with hash browns and toast for break-fast. Carrying eggs while bike camping would be nice, but not practical. I was on the road at 7 am. I passed through scenic farmland and small fishing towns along the coast. I took early morning pictures and posted them to Facebook. Sunrises and bike camping go together. I rode for a while without engaging the battery. The first leg of my ride was long, flat space along the waterfront. My bike was stuck in medium power, which was annoying because it drained the battery.

This would have been a problem, but it resolved itself a few days later. I am not sure how or why this happened. I rode all morning without the battery, and at 9 am I was in Montesano, Washington. I looked for a breakfast place, but nothing was open except a gas station. My second breakfast was chocolate donuts and a Rockstar. I washed them down, looking at my map. It was 92 degrees at 9 am. I wanted to charge my bike and make the next town before stopping for the day. I wanted to avoid extreme heat. I asked a few locals where I could camp. I was met with blank stares before someone saw my bike and stopped to chat.

He pointed up the hill to a county run campground. I could not find the place on Google Maps. I double-checked the site using my iPhone app and it too showed nothing. I left town to check out Sylvia Lake Park. I was glad I stopped. It was not planned and one of the better moves I made during my trip. The campsite was $10. They had showers and electricity. I had a nice spot in the forest overlooking a mountain lake. It was the town's hot spot. The whole town was here, it seemed. There were 200 people at the lake swimming, floating, sunbathing, and barbecuing.

I set up my campsite and met my neighbor, Kim. She had an interesting story of her own. We hit it off and became fast friends. I asked her to join me at the beach for the day in the sun. We grabbed our beach wear, floaties, towels, and headed to the beach. We spent the next few hours roasting in the sun and swimming in the cool mountain lake. I enjoyed the kids yelling and screaming, having water fights, and playing games. There were people fishing, kayaking, rowing, and rafting on the lake. Everyone was having fun in the sun on a picture-perfect Sunday.

I had a great day. I enjoyed the extra R&R rather than riding all day in the sun. I met a lot of new people. I listened to their stories and told some of my own. Everyone was amazed I had ridden my bicycle there. They encouraged me to finish my journey. I assured them I would. I was at the 1,000-mile mark and had no intention of stopping. Kim and I had a picnic lunch. She fed me fresh cherries, and I shared my iced Tang. We watched a family of bald eagles hunting and fishing for additional entertainment.

Kim and I talked for hours that night. She made dinner and seemed happy to have someone to cook for. She fed me spaghetti, which I ate in mass quantities. We had strawberries and cream for dessert. It was nice having company at night. Something I was not getting enough of, spending most of my trip alone. I went to bed with a full tummy and the comfort of a new friend. I left my bike charging outside the bathroom; I collected it before bedding down. It was 97%. I was happy and slept better for it.

I said goodnight to Kim, leaving early before she rose. I left her a goodbye note. My campsite was empty when she woke up. There is a moment of sadness when you meet someone special, share a day, a moment in time, knowing the next day they will be gone forever. Only a memory of something special, something fun, over as quickly as it started. One thing I've learned in life is that you meet people for a reason, whether planned or unplanned. You make a connection, share a bit of information which is passed on that never would have been if you did not stop and smell the roses. Engage others.

My day at Sylvia Lake State Park was one of those days. I will never forget it or Kim. I gained something from the decision, stopping for the day. Not traveling to my intended destination changed my outcome. You cannot predict your outcome until you do it, a quantum thought. That is the beauty of an adventure less planned. You decide, meet someone, get spaghetti, and talk till midnight.

Day 18
Monday, June 28, 2021

Kim was asleep as I rolled into the sunrise. I headed east for two hours. I was staring at the sun, engine stuck on medium. Wind at my back, I powered hard. I pulled into Schafer State Park to charge. I had to weigh the benefits of charging the battery fully over the rising heat. The longer I sat in the early morning shade, the higher the temperature rose. I could turn off the battery and ride without the engine, but I also ran the risk of getting stuck in the middle of nowhere. This is what eventually happened, but I had no idea at that time.

Schafer State Park is a beautiful campground southwest of Shelton, Washington. I charged my bike at the visitor kiosk. I used the bathroom and made breakfast at the visitor center. I wanted to get back on the road before the extreme heat made riding more difficult. I left an hour and 15 minutes later. I had 72%. With the power stuck on medium, l traveled fast but not far. If there was a day I needed low power, today was the day. On the hottest day of the year, I ran out of electricity. Luckily, it was flat.

I passed Lake Nashelle, and a town called Matlock. Matlock is not really a town but a postal address with a convenience store. There is nothing else. There is no place to charge your bike. I asked the convenience store employee and got a blank stare; I asked a local, and he pointed east toward Shelton. I left with a Monster energy drink and some Gatorade, which I turned into electricity of my own making. I rode past a large state prison and a racetrack that was open for motorcycles; I could not see them, but I heard race bikes traveling fast.

I rode without power for miles. I was at 15% and Shelton was miles away. It was super hot. The radio reported 118 degrees in Seattle. I was 75 miles from Seattle as the crow flies. I was inland, not near the water. I did not check the thermometer; my best guess was 110 degrees. I continued to ride in suffering heat and arrived at the "Canal" portion of the Puget Sound. I was heading due north when I arrived at my campground. I checked in, then spoke with a ranger who directed me to the hiker/biker area. I was extremely hot and dehydrated.

I realized something was not right with my body. My head and body were not acting in coordination, far from it. The trees were moving, and the road seemed to float. My balance was akin to a drunken person. To the uninitiated, these are signs of severe dehydration and heat exhaustion. It was 110 degrees in the shade, and I had ridden 55 miles. I was done in. I drank two large Gatorades, two large lemonades, one liter of water, and some salty snacks. It took an hour of sitting in the creek's cool waters and drinking a gallon of fluids for the trees to stop singing and the road to stop floating around. I recovered my senses enough to realize I had pushed myself too hard.

I spoke with a park ranger, explaining my symptoms. He seemed concerned, but I told him I was out of the woods. He said he would keep an eye on my bike if I wanted to go down to the water to cool off. I was sitting in the shade and felt much better, but his suggestion was good. I took him up on his offer. It was one o'clock in the afternoon. I went down to the Puget Sound and soaked in the canal. It did not look like a canal. The water was warm, 72 degrees. The air temperature was above 100, so it felt marvelous.

I went back to my campsite and continued to charge my phone and bike in an unoccupied RV site. I sat for an hour talking to a friend in San Francisco. This was the first time I mentioned not returning. My friend was surprised at my suggestion. The seed had been planted before I left California; now, in Washington, the seed was a plan. The plan was now public, out for scrutiny.

The first reaction was disbelief. Common with friends over the next week. I heard feedback and reservations from friends. I was questioned, and I gave answers. I took moving seriously and started planning accordingly. Moving was no longer a flight of fancy; it was a plan of action.

I went to bed that night with a heavy heart. I was looking for a home. Usually, this takes planning. Something done with forethought. I had two T-shirts, a pair of jeans, an extra pair of riding shorts, and a hoodie. I'd purchased rain gear, but everything I owned was in San Francisco. Most people who move do not leave everything they own at the point of departure. They pack and take it with them.

I had a tent, sleeping bag, and camping stove. Not much to start a new life with. Losing everything you own sucks. This had happened to me earlier in life. Losing everything should be avoided; since I was not planning to return, this was going to take some fancy footwork. I made plans to pay my rent and quit my job. This was not taken lightly. I took a month off work and planned to return. There was still food in my refrigerator. Now, things had changed.

After discussing this with Erika, I knew I was not going home. Sometimes, you are not sure until you verbalize your plans in public. I did not tell anyone of my intentions for a week. I did not contact my boss until I arrived in Alaska, secured a job, and rented an apartment. That night in Potlach State Park, after suffering near heat stroke and dehydration sickness, this was final. There was no turning back.

Day 19
Tuesday, June 29, 2021

Today, I rode up and down rolling hills along the southern part of Puget Sound. I rode for 30 miles with my battery stuck in medium power. This allowed me to travel fast but killed the battery. Without wind and moderate rolling hills, I traveled 30 miles in less than two hours. I stopped at a campground called Dosewallips and found an unoccupied RV site. I sat, charging my bike while eating noodles. The rangers stopped by while I was cooking. They enquired as to whether I was planning to stay at the campsite.

I explained, "I just needed to charge my bike for an hour or two." They asked the normal questions and were surprised I had traveled up the coast from San Francisco rather than down. I told them an e-bike levels the playing field with the wind. They seemed interested in e-bike touring. I told them it makes the ride enjoyable but also "it slows you down overall rather than speeding up your journey." If I had a solar charging system, it might be different. Stopping to charge and read a book does not make your journey efficient.

If I did not stop to recharge, it would have been faster. I would also have fewer opportunities to meet people. Sharing stories with other humans was part of the journey. The people I met, the places I stopped would be different. I would have buzzed through towns and cities without stopping and getting a taste of life. Often, it is the wrong turns or the sudden changes in plans that define our lives. It is not so much what happens but how you deal with events that happen when you make a "left at Albuquerque."

My adventure was not traveling the road but the hundreds of interactions with people I met on my trip. The people who gave me directions, let me use their garden hose, or allowed me to charge my battery, they are part of my story. There are hundreds of people with whom I interacted over the course of a month.

It was interactions that changed my journey from one of riding my bike to one of a thousand stories. I enjoy the interactions. They made my journey to Alaska worth writing about.

I spoke with a couple camping nearby, and they told me I had picked a bad site due to afternoon heat. I was blocked from the sun by trees facing east but not facing west and none above me. The couple explained they had been in the campsite I currently occupied. The thermometer had reached 112 degrees the day before. They expected the weather to remain hot today. I was not planning to stay; I was just charging my bike. I had ridden 30 miles by 10:30, and I was back on the road with approximately 75% battery two hours later. It was not that hot in the shade, but as I passed through sunny areas, I realized it was going to get very hot, very soon.

I rode another 16 miles and stopped at Lake Leland. I did

not plan on stopping so early. It was not even noon, but the thermometer was pushing 100 degrees, and my battery was at 36%. I could have kept riding, but Google Maps showed a campground nearby. I found the campground, found a self-pay site, and realized there were no electrical hookups in the campground. Not even in the bathrooms. I spoke with my neighbor Ed; he offered to charge my battery with his generator. I was hesitant at first but realized he wanted to help; it was not going to put him out. He was charging his fifth wheel anyway. I took him up on his offer and left the bike under his watchful eye. I changed into my bathing suit and headed for the lake.

I entered the water at a grassy area where people park their cars. I was surprised at how warm the water was. I knew the lake was fed by mountain streams from snow-capped mountains. The water was 78 degrees, bathtub warm. I used my camp mattress as a floaty and chatted with the locals. I spent two hours in the water. It was so hot you were overheating in a matter of minutes. I spent time quizzing locals on the economy in the area. What job prospects were there?

People talked candidly about the area. We talked about the housing situation. They explained housing costs; it was good information. Half the people I met lived in California at one point. Nobody talked about moving back. They either grew up there or had lived there. They did not say anything bad about California, except that it was unreasonably expensive. I agreed.

I made a small campfire that night and sat up writing notes and reading. I went to sleep early. It was still hot, but it had cooled off enough that I could crawl into my sleeping bag without sweating. The heat had taken its toll on me. I fell asleep without any trouble.

Day 20
Wednesday, June 30, 2021

I was up early to make an eighteen-mile trip to Port Townsend before it got windy, hot, or both. It was an interesting ride into Port Townsend. The Port is an old lumber mill town. I took the bike path winding through the outskirts of town, which paralleled the main road. The bike path was paved and dirt. It was early, so I passed joggers and a few dog walkers. I dropped down into the harbor area and asked a local where the ferry for Coupeville was located. He pointed north. I traveled north until I found the terminal. I waited my turn to purchase a ticket for the ferry. I pulled up to the vendor; he looked over my bike and trailer, then smiled and asked if I needed stowage.

It was funny because had I been a car or motorcycle with a trailer, I would have paid extra, but my little trailer got on free. Like a small child that travels for free, so did my trailer. I was told it would be a half hour. I found an electrical outlet while I was waiting. About 15 minutes later, a deckhand beckoned me and said they were ready for walk-ons. I guess my bicycle did not count as a vehicle. I walked on and parked my bike on the car deck. There was an electrical outlet next to my bike, so I asked if I could plug in. They shrugged and said I guess so. I took that as a yes and realized I was the first person to ever ask them. I might be the first e-biker to have charged on a ferry crossing.

The short hop over to Coupeville was uneventful. We left the dock and were a quarter mile out to sea before I realized we were moving. It was calm on the water. It was early, and with no wind, the water was still as a lake. I met people from the area and a few people passing through. We chatted about local events and the heat. When another bike rider asked me where I was going, I pointed north and told him I was heading for the border and hoped the Mounties would let me through.

Soon, everyone was giving me their opinion on the border closure with Canada. Everyone had a different viewpoint. There were a few Canadians on the boat that got stuck on the US side and were not allowed back into their own country. That seemed odd to me, but with Covid-19, it made sense.

By the time I got off the ferry, there were 20 people who shared time with me on the upper deck. They all waved goodbye and wished me luck. One person who had an RV told me about a campground 30 miles away called Cranberry Lake. He said it was a nice place, that he and his wife were heading there. I saw him later that day on the shoreline as I rowed by on a paddleboard. I had been trying to rent a kayak or a paddleboard since day two of my journey. Now on day 20, at the end of my journey, I'd finally found a lake that had a paddleboard rental. The big question was: paddleboard or kayak? I have ridden many kayaks, but never a paddleboard.

I chose the standup paddleboard and received a ten-second instruction by the vendor. Life jacket and a bottle of Gatorade in hand, I ventured out onto Cranberry Lake in Upstate Washington. It was fun; I paddled the whole lake, which was not very big. I enjoyed myself and added paddleboarding to my long list of sports. For hard-core adrenaline junkies, this is not your sport. For the weekend warrior and general couch potato, this is your sport. It is not very challenging, but it is fun. You can cruise around a lake quickly. I heard there are paddleboards for the ocean, which might be more exciting.

I went back to shore and met visitors passing through. They'd started in San Diego. I told them I rode from San Francisco. They were impressed with my feat. I had not thought much about how far I had ridden. I approached every day as a new journey with only a general idea of my daily destination. Whether or not I arrived at my intended destination did not matter. I needed to be in Bellingham the following day. The ferry left every Friday for Ketchikan, Alaska. I started thinking my trip was over. The Canadian border was still closed; they had announced opening the border July 5, 2021, but only to Canadian Citizens. I thought about the couple I'd met hours earlier on the Coupeville Ferry. They would be happy; but I was out of luck.

I looked at my map and planned my ride for the following day. Several people had warned me to "avoid Highway 11 into Bellingham." They said it was very narrow and curvy, that there would be traffic on it. There were two bicyclist that specifically told me they rode it once and would never do so again. They said it was too narrow and too dangerous for a bicyclist. Well, after looking at the map, I decided that Highway 11 was the only way into Bellingham from my current location. I would just have to leave extra early and try my luck.

The hiker/biker campground at Cranberry Lake was isolated from the rest of the sites. It was in no-man's-land. They had instituted a burn ban, which meant I was not allowed a campfire. I ended up cooking a steak on my stove, and three-quarters from medium rare the gas went. I now had a rare steak which ended up quite good. I added a little more salt than normal, then I ate it rare. The rare steak did not bother me; what bothered me was that I would have cold coffee in the morning. This seemed traumatic to me, but I remembered there was a gas station at the entrance to the park. I could pick up a green Monster. This seemed like a savior at the time.

As night approached, I grabbed my bike and went on an expedition. I rode randomly through the campgrounds to see what was there. I saw my ferry ride friends and waved as I passed. I found myself at lake's edge along the coastline. I sat at a picnic table and watched a spectacular sunset. As the sun sank into the sea that night, I thought about tomorrow being my last day of riding. I would travel the rest of the way to Alaska on the Alaska Marine Highway ferry. Things turned out much differently, but at the time I did not know this.

Day 21
Thursday, July 1, 2021

The first omen of the day was cold coffee. Instant crystals did not dissolve in cold water. Along the Northern Pacific coast, the temperature drops to the low fifties at night. It had been warm until the onshore breeze had picked up the night before. Cold instant coffee with chunky undissolved crystals is not a good way to start your day. No Quaker Oats to feel warm and homey either. I would grab a Monster at the gas station; I should have known better. My brain did not process that the gas station was closed at 5 am. It was 5:15 am when I rode past the dark station.

The chunky dark coffee crystals finally dissolved after five miles. I rode without electricity to warm my bones and muscles. It was a beautiful morning with zero wind. I crossed "Deception Pass" and rode along a busy highway that had a shoulder as wide as a standard car lane. Only problem was the road was turning into a two-lane highway with a lot of traffic. People were heading to work. I was now in a populated area. I had taken the scenic route with fewer people and traffic. Debris, rocks, pebbles, chunks of wood, sticks, glass, nails, cans, and bottles were everywhere. I dipped and dodged. I was traveling quickly, trying to stay visible to oncoming traffic. It slowly became unnerving in the early morning commute.

I pulled into a gas station to grab a Monster and chocolate donuts. I needed a quick pick-me-up. At 7:30 am, the gas station attendant took one look at me and said, "Please be careful out there." I was taken off guard and did not realize she was speaking to me. I was in my biking gear. She then went on to say, "Cars in this area do not respect bicyclists, so remain extra cautious." I appreciated her concern. It was dangerous along the shoulder; she was obviously from the area and spoke from the heart. I told her I would be careful. I was turning left and heading north in two miles. She asked which road, and I told her. She said it was better than the freeway, but I should still be careful.

I thanked her. I was deeply touched by the sentiment of a total stranger. She looked right at me like she knew me, but we had never met. Her warning became apparent quickly. She was correct; it was dangerous. I knew without her telling me. It was the only road through the area; a bike path would have been heaven-sent. The area was crisscrossed with waterways, streams, gullies, and irrigation canals. The highway was the only way to cross from point A to point B.

I made a left turn and got off the main road. The next few miles went through a peaceful area populated with cows. Feeling lonely, I said hello to the cows. They seemed interested; they stopped what they were doing and stared. Their demeanor made me feel like a rockstar. My fans took great interest in my passing their pastures. The chocolate donuts and Monster did the job of picking up my energy and spirits. I felt good, so I rode hard intermittently with the power on and off.

I passed Edison, Washington. Somehow, I missed my turn and ended up at a dead-end near an art studio. It was not scary. This was the right place to make a wrong turn, so I made little effort to find my way back. I took in the scene and pedaled through town. I saw a breakfast spot and thought about stopping. I looked for an easy electrical hookup; seeing none, I kept riding. I still had 40% of my battery but knew I should top off before attempting Highway 11. People had warned me not to ride the road, so I wanted to have full power if necessary.

I was about to leave Edison; I passed a roadside drive-through coffee shack. There was a post office and shop in the area. I pulled in, circled the post office looking for an electrical outlet. I did not see one, but passing the shop, I saw an electrical plug in the rafters. I was getting good at spotting electrical outlets. I stopped and plugged my charger into the roof. The charger hung in the air and dangled down from the rafters, two feet above my bike. It was not discreet, but I plugged in anyway. I sat there reading my book and waiting patiently for the car at the coffee stand to move along so I could get a cup. Twenty minutes later, I realized the car and the proprietor of the coffee shack must be friends because she had not moved. I walked over and interrupted them; I wanted a cup of coffee.

The car owner was the store owner whom I was "borrowing electricity from." I had not been paying attention either, because the store turned out to be the local gun shop. The lady in the car told me it was ok. I charged my battery, and she promised not to shoot me. That was a good deal. Now, with a warm cup of coffee, I returned to the bench in front of the gun shop. I read my book. It felt good sitting there reading, watching the town come to life. The cows loved me, the gun shop was not shooting at me, life was good. I charged my bike for free without fear of drive-by shootings. These details can be missed by humans if they are not attentive. It is often small details—like not being used for target practice—that make things interesting.

After charging to 60%, I remounted, said thank you to the shop owner and the coffee barista, and rode off into the sunlight. Next stop, Highway 11. I contemplated the dangers. I had been warned twice in different locations to avoid Highway 11. I'd also received a warning two hours earlier from the gas station attendant. I looked at the map; to go around was a detour twice as far as the proposed route. I was not in a rush, as I had 25 miles to my destination. I had 60% of my battery, but the elevation gain would drain that to 25% over the next 10 miles. I decided to risk it and determined I made the right decision.

All things in life are relative to what you have previously experienced. Highway 11 is narrow and curvy in places. Going uphill on a bike is fraught with danger. Blind curves and cars traveling 35 mph do not mix well. I used my second power setting and rode defensively. I had no problem getting to the top of the pass. I found Highway 11 to be a six on a scale of one to ten, with a one being least scary and a ten representing hell on wheels. I had ridden a few nines and one ten on my journey. This was nothing compared to some of the roads. It was beautiful and worth the occasional nuisance of a truck passing with little to no shoulder. I grew up on roads like this and found them pleasing.

I enjoyed myself and pulled into Larrabee State Park. I used the ranger station's electrical outlet to charge my battery. I made a light lunch and relaxed, then read for another hour and a half before I got back on the road. I had 15 miles to go before I reached the Bellingham Ferry terminal. I was in the middle of a forest, at peace with the world at that moment. I felt good. I felt a sense of harmony with my ride, with nature, my body, mind, and soul. I sat in the park with a sliver of sunshine breaking through the trees. I remembered playing in sunspots coming through the window as a child. I was warm in my ray of sunshine. I sat quietly without reading, writing, or distractions and just felt good.

I got back on my bike; I had plenty of battery for the next 15 miles. I was not worried about running out of electricity. Pumping my legs and getting the bike to 25 mph felt great. I exited the "not so dangerous" road and flew into Bellingham at 20 mph. It felt good, so I did not slow down until I hit a stoplight.

I missed my turn to the ferry building. I was surprised when I checked Google Maps. I'd passed it two miles back. I turned around and ended up at the ferry building 10 minutes later. I was not in a rush, enthralled with the small city of Bellingham. I love exploring new towns. Bellingham is a modern city with an old town feel.

I parked my bike outside the ferry terminal and found an electrical outlet by the front door. I went inside and was perplexed at the lack of activity. I quickly realized why there was no activity. I'd read 20 blogs regarding the Alaska Marine Highway System (AMHS). I had visited what I thought was their website, but it was an advertisement by a third-party vendor. The third-party vendor had not updated their website because it had gone out of business. I had no way of knowing AMHS had changed departure times. I'd read 20 stories on the internet that said the ferry left every Friday afternoon. I saw tickets offered for sale on the website for Friday. I assumed it still left every Friday afternoon.

I was wrong. I'd timed my arrival the day before the ferry left. I'd planned to get a hotel room in town that night and board the ferry with clean clothes, having showered, shaved, and shined. Not to be. The ferry had changed its departure date to Wednesday. I'd missed the ferry by one day. I was heartbroken, miserable at that moment. I rode into Bellingham feeling like a champion finishing the Tour de France, only to end up feeling like the Tour de Fool. I sat there in shock for 20 minutes. The next ferry left in six days; the Canadian border was still closed.

No other options were available to me. I was completely despondent. I walked around, asking if it was true. I was a day late. I was not mistaken. I thought I had planned it perfectly. I could have ridden 15 more miles the past three days. Riding an extra 15 miles a day would have gotten me to the ferry terminal a day early. The ferry made a big loop and left from Bellingham once a week. I sat in stunned silence for another 30 minutes.

I did not know what to do as the shock of making such a monumental error in calculation hit me full force. I looked out at the empty dock space where the ferry should have been parked and decided not to decide anything until I had a good night's sleep. I asked around for local motels in the area. One of the AMHS workers heard my plight and gave me direction to a decent motel. He did me a favor. I rode east into the heart of town and found a small locally owned motel that had rooms for $65 a night. I checked in and took a 45-minute shower and came out refreshed.

I turned on the television for the first time in eight days. I caught up on world events and relished the air conditioning. I was inside for the first time in quite a while. I quickly decided I did not like tomorrow's 10 am checkout time and went to pay for another night so I could sleep in and relax. I told myself not to worry or even think about what I was going to do next. Now that my plans had blown up, I told myself to relax and enjoy the day. I thought the end of my ride was a failure. I could not have been more wrong.

I put on clean clothes and ordered a large pizza. I walked to the pizza shop and picked up the pizza and a liter of Coca-Cola. I went back to my air-conditioned motel room and listened to kids playing in the pool while gorging on pizza. It was a magical pizza because I was glowing and completely content. I was peaceful again. All my despair from making a stupid logistical error dissipated. I was happy. I fell asleep early with the news on. I watched stories on forest fires in the areas I had passed through days ago. I said a prayer for the trees and slept soundly.

Day 22
Friday, July 2, 2021

After getting up every day for the past three weeks at 4:30 am, I enjoyed getting up at 10 am. I made coffee at the hotel's coffee maker. I was not sure which was worse—my instant or the hotel's coffee. I watched TV with the air conditioning on, lying under the covers while reading the newspaper, drinking coffee, doing as little as possible. At one in the afternoon, I walked down to the shopping mall, visiting the REI store. I'd purchased my bike camping equipment at REI in San Francisco. My sleeping bag, camping stove, mattress, lantern, and assorted accessories were all REI. I bought parts for my bike and fuel for my camp stove. I stopped at a Thai restaurant and ate a large bowl of spicy noodles. I was now stuffed and loaded down with purchases from REI and Safeway. I waddled back to my hotel. I did laundry, then organized my notes on my trip.

Later that evening, I walked to the local café, ordered fish and chips for dinner. I walked back to my hotel room; I passed several kids riding their bikes in the evening heat without parents around. In San Francisco and the immediate areas around the city, you do not see kids playing in the street. It dawned on me as I watched them that this made me feel good. Seeing kids playing outside was normal when I grew up. We did not have Xboxes, PlayStations, or Nintendo. We went outside to play kickball, football, baseball in the street. We made our own games and played until the sun went down or our parents called us home for dinner. That was normal behavior. I wondered when and why the world had changed so much. Were people really so rotten that kids could not play by themselves or explore, playing physical games rather than mental ones?

I do not believe humanity has changed, but our perception of it has. I do not think bad things happen to children more now than they did in the past. What has changed is that there are more children in the world for bad things to happen to, and we now have the ability to notify the world via the internet. We hear about it; mass media rather than the prevalence of malice has increased. If a child disappears, the whole world knows in minutes. The Amber Alert system is well known in the United States. I doubt it is different in other countries. Bad things happen, but as a percentage of the population, has crime really increased? I do not think so, but I could be wrong. How we deal with it and how quickly it is reported has changed, though.

I did not ride my bike at all today, a first in several months. I rode for three weeks, but trained for months before leaving. Even if it was 10 or 20 miles, I rode every day. I thought about this as I climbed into bed. I went to bed early, watching television. Something I rarely do, even when home. I just do not watch television; I use it as a sleeping pill. I turn it on, and 20 minutes later, I am asleep. My sleeping pill worked its wonders, and I was out like a light. The only thing I accomplished other than washing my clothes was my battle plan for reaching Alaska.

My original idea was shot down by Covid-19 restrictions in Canada. They closed their borders not just to e-bikers named Steve, but everyone. My plan, crossing over to Victoria Island, was out. Taking the inland route, riding to Prince Rupert, was out as well. I was at the end of the road. I decided to ride to the Canadian Border and yell at the Mounties. I wanted to tell them I was vaccinated. I thought I could change their mind; I was wrong.

I spent the rest of the night investigating job opportunities and places to live. I liked Bellingham. There is a collegiate feel, vibrant and youthful. Lots of young people in the area. They had the summer off, were out having fun. I located the real Alaska Marine Highway System website. They had a help wanted sign and were actively recruiting. A job with the State of Alaska sounded interesting. This would be a great place to work if I wanted to see Alaska. I could earn money while traveling. It was two weeks on, two weeks off. That would give me plenty of time to write and finish my travel guide. I stayed up late researching the job. There were a lot of qualifications and licenses I needed. The list was long; it would not be easy. For some reason, it seemed like the right thing to do; I applied. I went to bed feeling better about what I was now planning to do.

Day 23
Saturday, July 3, 2021

I left that morning with a new appreciation for Bellingham. I was there for a day and a half, already calling it home. Strange way to look at things, but I knew I would be back soon enough.

There is a campground a few miles from the Canadian border, so I decided to go there and rest a few days before returning to Bellingham. I went to the grocery store, purchasing supplies for the weekend. It was Fourth of July. I bought steak, potato chips, nonalcoholic beer, and corn on the cob. I packed carefully; I was carrying 15 extra pounds of food, as buying groceries a day at a time helped keep the weight down. I headed for Birch Bay Campground. It was an easy forty-mile ride.

I rode through small towns and crossed a river. I found myself on the coast, in the vicinity of a large oil refinery. I saw "help wanted" signs everywhere. It seemed normal for every business to have a "help wanted" sign. How could every business need help? And I mean every business.

I arrived at the campground before noon. A sign in the ranger station window said "Open at 2 pm due to Covid-19 manpower shortage." I asked campers where the hiker/biker site was, and they seemed confused. They said there was none. I disagreed with them but was nice about it. I was right, there is a hiker/biker site at Birch Bay State Park. It is isolated from the other sites. I understood how someone might not know they existed. The campsite did not have water or electricity. It was close to the ocean, but also close to a freshwater drainage ditch.

The swamp, I affectionally called it. A creek turned into a canal that dead-ended into a swamp. During a rainstorm or high tide, it would flush out. The swamp did neither during the time I spent there. I stayed for three days; a decision made by default. I needed a place to relax for a few days before I went back to Bellingham. I made camp and left my camping gear, lightening my load by 40 pounds. I found a spot to charge my bike before heading to the border.

I rode up the coast to the Canadian border. I rode the length of Birch Bay, a beautiful bay surrounded by beach homes. The town was crowded, but I was unaware of the reasons for all the excitement. I knew it was the Fourth of July weekend; however, I did not know this was the fireworks capital of Washington State. I exaggerate, but as I rode through the sleepy town filled with weekend warriors camping, partying, sunbathing, eating, drinking, and being merry Americans, the place was transforming into a fireworks extravaganza.

I passed through Blaine and arrived at Peace Arch State Park. This was it, the end of the line—the Canadian border. I went down to the arch and took pictures. I was not supposed to go on the other side of the arch, which meant entering Canada. I had come to yell at the Mounties, ignoring the signs and locals waving me off. I traveled into Canada, stopped a hundred yards in, and took more pictures. I was in no-man's-land. I was the only person in the area. I could feel a thousand eyes on me. I took a few hasty pictures and headed back to America. I never yelled at the Mounties, but I did get a stare down by a stern-faced US Border Patrol agent, who said, "Don't do that again." I got the message and went to find ice cream to celebrate the "end of the line."

There was a party at Peace Arch State Park. It was Saturday, July 3; people from all over the USA had come to the demarcation line to see loved ones from across the border. There is an area the US Border Patrol agents keep an eye on. They were using facial recognition software. There were cameras everywhere. I am sure there was a considerable array of monitoring equipment watching the crowd because there is no wall at Peace Arch Park. You can walk into the US or Canada. I do not know how far you could go without being arrested. If you were in the park, the authorities turned a blind to the comings and goings of residents from both sides. At the end of the day, you had to be on your side of the border.

I did not realize how many personal relationships had been severed due to Covid-19. Husbands and wives working on opposite sides of the border had been separated as well as boyfriends and girlfriends. They met in the middle of Peace

Arch Park. Couples set up tents for the comingling of relations. It was good to see happy people. People temporarily interrupted from normal routines back together again.

I rode 10 miles back to Birch Bay Campground. I made dinner while dwelling on the isolated campsite. Moments later, I heard a group of people heading down the hill. A large group site with a permanent overhang shelter was next to the hiker/biker area. My neighbors were loud. They set up tents the size of condominium complexes. I have never seen tents so large in my life. There were only 20 people in their group, but a rowdy group they were. They kept me up till 2:30 am. I was going to introduce myself, but I chose to read and relax in my tent instead. Sleep was impossible, as the group kept up their chatter until 2 am. I was not mad; I did not have to get up early. I was staying to enjoy the Fourth of July.

<h3 style="text-align:center">Day 24
Sunday, July 4, 2021</h3>

The Fourth of July is my second favorite holiday after Groundhog Day. I love summertime activities. We always had fireworks at the end of the day. I love fireworks and continue to enjoy the Fourth of July. I had no plans, nor any idea where I would be on the Fourth of July. If the Canadian border had been open, I would have been on Victoria Island in Canada. I would not have participated in the Fourth of July activities because there are none in Canada. I got up at 7:30 am, made coffee. I'd spotted a café the day before, so rather than make breakfast, I planned to go there for brunch. I took snacks, my beach towel, my floaties, and sunblock to the beach. I rode towards town, grabbing a picnic table next to a large Vietnamese family. They viewed me warily at first, but I waved as they made haste to go clamming along the tideline. I was fascinated with their activity. They worked together and alone. Some of the kids took great pride in digging up clams and mussels.

I eventually went down to the shoreline, leaving my bike and backpack to the watchful eyes of two Vietnamese ladies. They were in their eighties and the matriarchs of the family. After sitting next to them for two hours, reading my book, and snacking on chips, I knew them, and they knew me. I pointed to my bike on the way out to the tideline, and they nodded in unison. No language barrier here. They understood the implicit duty to watch my bike. I spent an hour swimming and watching them hunt shellfish. They knew their clams. They found many oysters, and mussels too.

I was surprised by how warm the water was. The water is warmer in Birch Bay than in San Francisco. Birch Bay is shallow; the currents keep the water trapped and warm. You can walk a hundred yards out and still touch bottom. It is a great bay for swimming.

I went to shore, giving the two matriarchs a polite bow with both hands pressed together as a thank you. I received gracious smiles in return. As I said, no language barrier. We understood each other perfectly. I collected 40 mussels and a couple of clams myself. I did not have any equipment and had to use my bare hands to dig my mollusks. It was now lunchtime, so I went back to my campsite and boiled water, then added butter, salt, garlic, and my mollusks. I had buttered rolls with a bowl of steamers. I was proud of myself, foraging my lunch. I ventured into the brambles and collected an assortment of blackberries, blueberries, and salmonberries. I felt good about foraging my food. I had accomplished something special. When was the last time you hunted your own food for a meal? I remember as a child having a garden. We collected fruits and vegetables to accompany our dinner. But a whole meal?

I changed my brunch in town to an early dinner. With a big smile and a full tummy, I rode past bungalows and condominiums. There were lawn chairs facing the street. There was going to be a town parade. I was not disappointed. The parade was typical small-town Fourth of July. I met people, engaged in small talk. People asked about my e-bike; how far, fast it could go. I told kids it went 50 mph for 100 miles; they were impressed. I told the adults that it went 28 mph for 45 miles before it needed a recharge. The kids were fascinated with a 50-mph bike; they were ten years away from getting a driver's license and had no concept of what 50 mph meant. I was their hero, but lying to children is inappropriate behavior. No matter how much fun it is and how innocent you are. I hope they forgive when they realize I was pulling their leg.

I watched the parade and found myself at the wrong end of Birch Bay. I was hungry now, but on the opposite side of town. I watched the parade to its conclusion. At 3 pm, I ordered a nonalcoholic beer and a burger at the café. There was a wait for tables, so I offered seats to two ladies. I had a four-top and the wait was long. We chatted about life in Washington state.

They had driven from Bellingham for the Fourth of July. They said this was the place to be. I thought they were kidding. I'd thought of riding 20 miles to Bellingham to watch fireworks; many gatherings were canceled, so this was good news. Birch Bay is a small town; I inquired, "Could it be true?" The ladies looked at me and said, "Wait and see."

I was not disappointed. I am a fireworks aficionado; I have seen the largest fireworks shows ever produced. I saw the best fireworks show I have ever seen in Birch Bay. There was no public event, but there were hundreds of private party fireworks around the six-mile cove. Every hundred yards, a family or group of families banded together to light fireworks. It was incredible. I have never seen anything like it. I participated vicariously through others. They started before sunset and did not stop until 2 am. I moved around a few times on my bike. I ended up on a private beach sitting with two large families. I met a lady who ran a fireworks stand nearby. It was located on the Native American reservation, tribal land not subject to state restrictions.

She explained how they worked and the cost. She said with authority that the displays we saw cost tens of thousands of dollars. She said the individual displays cost five to ten thousand; others more elaborate were sponsored by local businesses as far south as Everett. She said families from as far away as Spokane, Washington, came every summer. I was overwhelmed by the volume of fireworks. It was amazing.

I left the show after two hours. My oohs and aahs tired me out. I went to bed two miles away as the booming abated. I was satiated and fell asleep a happy man. I'd foraged my own meal, had dinner with two beautiful women, and watched awesome fireworks. That is my definition of a good day—one for the books of unexpected fun and frolicking. I planned nothing and did everything.

Day 25
Monday, July 5, 2021

I woke late, as it was a holiday. I had nothing to do, not in a rush to do anything. I got out of my sleeping bag at 9 am, which seemed like the middle of the day. I made coffee and oatmeal for breakfast. My noisy neighbors had been drowned out last night by fireworks. I watched them take down three tents the size of a condominium complex. It was interesting. What took them hours to set up took 10 minutes to break down. With the tent city decommissioned, I said goodbye to my neighbors. I never barked at them for keeping me up till 3 am, which was good because they were nice people. Their pilgrimage was an annual event, so be warned if you head there on the Fourth of July. Anyone who owns tents that big needs to use them at least once a year.

I went down to the picnic table I'd claimed the previous day. I missed my Vietnamese neighbors. They had left quietly in the morning; by noon, the campground was empty. I was left with the remnants of fun and frolicking the night before. I toured Birch Bay and saw remnants of thousands upon thousands of rockets and explosive devices. The people who participated were trash sensitive. Everything was bagged and deposited at the curb. I wondered who organized it, or was it a spontaneous act? I rode the five-mile curve of Birch Bay and saw a handful of trash that had not been bagged. I was impressed. It was 11 am, and the area was clean. I imagined somebody had organized it years ago. There were thousands of people, and the place was spotless. I did not see a sign to pick up after yourself. Had they left the trash in situ, it would have taken a hundred people two days to collect it all. Fireworks make a mess. So do picnic baskets, beer cans, and sodas, but the place was spotless.

I finished *The Girl with the Dragon Tattoo*, which I'd started in Elk, California. I get distressed when I finish a book. I slow down my reading and wonder if I am the only one who hates finishing a book because I miss the characters. I'd met a young lady riding her bike the day before. She was local, so I asked her where I could get used books. She told me about a little library kiosk a mile down the road. I must have passed it two or three times; it was right next to the pink houses. I was mesmerized by the little pink houses. In honor of my favorite song by John Mellencamp, "Little Pink Houses," I stopped and took pictures of the pink houses. I also picked up a book.

I got Sidney Sheldon's *Doomsday Conspiracy*, a spy novel that states coincidences should be viewed with suspicion, and if they continue to happen, that is a harbinger of malice. Since coincidences keep happening, I assume this is not good. Everything is connected in some way. It seems every person I meet is part of a large puzzle called life. Each event has bearing on which direction I go next.

Have you had a coincidence that stops you in your tracks? Ask yourself, "How did they know that?" or "Why did that just happen?" The book I chose at random explains coincidences in an evil way. My coincidences are piling up at an alarming rate. People tell me stories that have a direct bearing on my life. Like Hansel and Gretel leaving a trail of breadcrumbs as I travel north. If I veer off in the wrong direction, something nudges me back in the right direction, or is it the wrong direction? Part of life's great mystery. You do not know until you venture down the rabbit hole. The problem is some roads, once traveled, cannot be undone.

I went to bed thinking about my future. Tomorrow's ride back to Bellingham. An easy ride, so I stayed up late reading my book. I was looking forward to the ride. The last three days had been R&R. I ate hot dogs for dinner and picked some berries for dessert.

Day 26
Tuesday, July 6, 2021

I was up at 5 am and left after breakfast; I was not traveling far. My destination was fixed. I wanted to be within crawling distance of the AMHS ferry terminal in Bellingham, Washington. What I mean is, if anything went wrong with my bike or trailer, I could walk to the ferry. I had ridden this far, so I was determined to board it this time.

I was on the road at 6:15 am and backtracked the way I'd come to Birch Bay. At the first crossroads, I decided to explore the area. There were several routes to Bellingham. I'd traveled one route on my way up; I choose a different one on the way back. Part of my ride went through an area I had already traversed, but there was no choice in the matter due to a bridge. I had a river to cross, and there was only one bridge. At the next juncture, I detoured onto a new road.

I passed suburbs and enjoyed seeing Bellingham. I used Google Maps to navigate through town. Google Maps directed me to the Interurban Trail. I was a little skeptical. Not to criticize Google Maps, but it had gotten me in trouble several times. To be fair, it had rescued me from trouble an equal number of times. The Interurban Trail could be good or bad. It was 8 am; if I got lost, I could backtrack, so I took the trail. I was glad I did.

This was a highlight of my ride. They built an incredible trail through Bellingham, Washington. I thank the city planners; it is a trail of beauty. Worth its weight in gold. I traveled for several miles and was sad when I exited onto Highway 11. I did not have far to go from there.

To describe the Interurban Trail would be an injustice; you need to ride it. The size of a fire road, unpaved, and a work of beauty that wanders through the woods and backyards of homes. I passed joggers, dog walkers, and a few bikers. Worth going out of your way to visit. I encourage city planners to travel the Interurban Trail to see what a simple idea and planning can do for mankind. It is forward-thinking that makes the world a better place to live. You can tell how much I loved the trail; it is incredible.

I arrived at Larrabee State Park at 9 am. I found the hiker/biker site; it was nice, but the whole park is beautiful. I took the first site I came across, which turned out to be the only spot available. I paid the fee at the ranger station. I went to the main campground and found an empty RV site with electricity. I plugged in my bike and left it charging. I changed into my bathing suit and walked to the beach.

If you visit Larrabee Park, go to the beach. I walked down a steep path to a rocky beach. I met Audrey and her daughter Trail, who were hanging out on the beach. We exchanged stories and talked about historical fiction. We'd read the same books. I was in bookaholic heaven, talking about books all day, finding someone who shares my passion. I went swimming and played with sea anemones in tidal pools and had a great day. I watched kids being kids, building sandcastles on a rocky beach. They swam, played frisbee, football, and paddleball.

I spent a few heaven-sent hours in the sun, just being a kid again. At 3 pm, I needed nourishment, so I packed up my bag, and off I went.

I said goodbye to my new friends, walked back to my campsite. I detoured on the way back and ended up scaling a thirty-foot rock that landed me on the railroad tracks. I walked the tracks, trying to balance on one track for as long as I could. Sounds easy; I got the hang of it quickly. Watching kids brought back the kid in me. I made a game of walking the track. I heard the train long before I saw it. I felt the vibration through my sandals. I had no intention of playing tag with the train. I was off to one side as the lumbering giant plowed the tracks.

Most of us have seen trains from the safety of our cars, but when a train comes rumbling by, you realize how huge and powerful these machines are. You feel the world tremble around you. The noise penetrates your body. Trains are loud and very heavy, an impressive sight to see. The conductor tooted his horn to warn me, which left an indelible mark on my body. Loud is not the right word; penetrating is closer to the mark.

The train passed; I jumped a fence to get into the camp-ground. My site was on the other side. I felt trains as they passed my campsite all night. I was told to expect at least one train per hour. I was surprised the track was active, but even during Covid-19, transportation did not stop. People need food, beverages, and goods that make the modern world tick. My neighbor's four- and five-year-old kids kept me entertained. I answered their questions under the watchful eye of the father. I got the impression their trip was to give mom some rest and dad a chance to spend time with his daughters. I could be wrong; they were incredibly polite, and the father taught "please and thank you" at the appropriate times.

I was impressed with my neighbor's kids. When you do not have your own, you have a different view of child-rearing. Whether right or wrong, I love watching family dynamics. I love seeing kids being kids. When you live in a big city, you do not see these daily interactions. You do not see kids playing in the street anymore. It is dangerous, so you never see unattended children in the city. It was nice to see kids playing without parental involvement. It takes on a whole new dynamic.

I went to bed reading my book. I needed a new book before boarding the ferry the next day. I was excited and stayed up late reading by lantern. I heard the train rumble by a hundred yards away, felt the ground vibrate as I drifted off. I woke up at 1 am, turned off my lantern, and peeled the book from my forehead before I went back to sleep.

Day 27
Wednesday, July 7, 2021

Nervous energy abounds. I was up at 5:15 am, on the road to the ferry terminal shortly thereafter. It was 10 miles away. I made the ride easy, using more electricity than needed. I arrived before it opened. I was first in the ticket line, the only one actually. I watched staff unload luggage and people pick up family members. I was on nervous energy, an excited energy high. I felt alive but anxious. My one-way ticket cost me $508.

I had enough money to buy a round-trip ticket, but if I liked Ketchikan, I was going to stay. I'd left San Francisco with a $100 a day budget. I had $3,000 for my trip. I'd spent $25 a day on average, which included my campsites and food. I'd purchased equipment and clothing: a raincoat at the North Face Outlet, new tires for the cart, and a tent in Fort Bragg, California. I'd spent a few hundred on hotel rooms along the way, but I'd been under budget until now. I'd just busted the budget. I was not worried. I had savings, but I was trying to stay on budget. This left me with $300 of my original $3,000. My original plan was to ride to Prince Rupert and take the ferry from there. This would have been much cheaper. On return, I was planning to pack up the bike and fly home. I planned $150 for the ferry ride from Prince Rupert to Ketchikan and $500 on the flight home.

So much for budgets and plans. I threw out the idea before I crossed the river to Washington. From that point on, I knew this was a one-way journey. I was no longer worried. I had enough savings to pay the first month's rent, last month's rent, and a deposit for an apartment. I would get a job when I arrived. I left home with a pair of jeans, two pairs of riding shorts, two T-shirts, and my favorite pair of Nike Airs. I had no regular clothes or household goods. I'd left everything I owned back in San Francisco.

I had a lot on my mind. I found a place to charge my bike and went to the grocery store. I bought $150 worth of groceries in Bellingham. I went to the bookstore and bought two books for the ferry ride. Sidney Sheldon was finished. I had several hours to wait before we loaded. I'd arrived eight hours early and had used the time to research Ketchikan housing.

At 2 pm, another bicyclist showed up for the ferry. His bike was modified for touring. His equipment was on the light side, self-contained. I introduced myself, making friends with JC quickly. He had stories to tell, and I told mine. We discussed aspects of riding. He was heading for the Dalton Highway, which parallels the Alaskan Pipeline, a daunting ride for any biker. There are no services for hundreds of miles. You need solar or a battery pack lasting 200 miles to e-bike. We talked nonstop and boarded the ferry together.

The ferry ride was incredible. We found lounge chairs in the solarium, a glass-enclosed area on the top deck. There is also an area for tents. Bring duct tape if you pitch a tent; stakes do not work on steel decks. Our spot was blocked from wind. Nighttime was chilly, but heat lamps helped. The view was incredible and the general excitement intoxicating, with the sunset after midnight, dawn three hours away. In the northern latitudes, summer days are 20 hours, adding to the surreal atmosphere.

It is difficult to explain how I felt as I ventured north. Never been to Alaska, never seen the inside passage, and never a sunset after midnight. Twilight lasted past 1 am and sunrise at 4 am. It was beautiful; I was intoxicated by sunlight, a sensory overload. I slept a couple of hours the following day. The ferry ride was 38 hours. It went by fast, as I was enthralled with the view and events unfolding before me. I saw whales, dolphins, and eagles soaring overhead, adding overwhelming sensations. We passed small colorful villages, fishing vessels, and tugboats. I slept four hours in total but did not feel tired. There was too much to see and do. I explored the ship and loved everything.

I went to the restaurant to experience the scene. The ferry was not filled, due to Covid-19, but there were enough passengers to keep me entertained with new stories. I love meeting people when traveling. People are more willing to tell their stories away from home. For the inquisitive and precocious self, this was Disneyland. I guess some of us never grow out of childhood curiosity. I love new people, places, and things. If there is someone new to talk to or new to see, there I am, right in the middle.

I am not shy. I am a communicator. I bring diverse sets of individuals to the party. I met 70 people and knew half on a first-name basis by the time we disembarked. I enjoyed the ride north; I wanted to stay and see what was next.

I'd purchased a ticket to Ketchikan, Alaska, so it was time to disembark. My friend JC, who was traveling further north, had a three-day layover in Ketchikan. He needed a different ferry to take him to Whittier, Alaska. He booked a local hotel room; I had no plans, no place to stay. We split the hotel room and saw the town. For the next three days, I explored the sights. I saw totem poles, the Civic Center, Town Hall, Recreation Center, docks, and harbors. I traveled north and south along the main road. I went inland. When JC left, I decided to stay permanently. I started the process of finding an apartment.

Third day, I still had no place to live. I found a campground for the night on a beautiful lake north of Ward Cove. I used the internet, searching for permanent accommodations. I talked to people in town, asking where I could rent an apartment. On Sunday, the town was empty, most of the businesses closed until noon. Back in town eating lunch at a picnic table, I picked up the local paper. I saw personals, help wanted ads, and on the last page, a listing of rentals. I scanned down the page and found a single listing for a studio. I called the number, surprised to get a real person who happened to be three blocks away. He gave me directions, and five minutes later, I was sitting in his living room discussing rental agreements.

The price was right, the down payment reasonable. I needed to dip into savings to foot the bill, but this was not an expense of my journey. This was a living expense. Inevitable no matter where you live; if I wanted to stay, I had to pay the rent. I needed a day to sleep on it; he said ok. In the backyard, there were two kids fishing. They caught several king salmon. I bought one and took it back to my campsite.

Later that night, I ate grilled salmon, organized my thoughts and finances, and made the decision. That was a monumental, life-changing event. When I started my ride, I was on a bucket-list mission to see my fiftieth state, with every intention of returning home. No intentions of staying in Alaska. Now I was in Alaska with no plans, no job, no place to live—things normal people consider before they move 1,700 miles. I'd left critical paperwork, my social security card, birth certificate, etc. I'd left my clothes, computers, electronics, tools, furniture, bedding, everything, in San Francisco. I had the clothes on my back; luckily, it was summer, because I had the lightest clothes possible. This was Alaska, so shorts and a T-shirt were not going to work.

My decision to stay brought complications. I sat alone at Ward Lake, thinking life is too short to be indecisive. This was my chance to change my life. What did I want to do with the rest of my life? Not an easy question. What were my goals for the next ten years? Number one goal: to be happy, healthy, and live life to its fullest. With my passion for reading and writing, there was no reason I could not read and write in Alaska. I looked down at my Nikes; just do it. I did.

Before I left, I started writing a book. There is a better chance of me finishing it in Alaska than in San Francisco, I thought. Writing is hard work. You get paid when you produce something. It can take years; try living on nothing for years. I write blogs on the internet, getting paid for content. I am not a published author, but if you are reading this, then you can check that off my bucket list. I realized in the quiet, calm night that this is where I am supposed to be. I vowed I would stay in Ketchikan, Alaska, until I did two things.

One is to write the book you are now reading. Two is to get it published. One way or another, I was not leaving anytime soon. I got my priorities in order. Sign the apartment lease, obtain a job, get my Merchant Mariner Credentials (MMC), and write every day. I needed a job that would not interfere with my writing. I wanted a day job, nine to five, so I could eat dinner and write. I needed an internet connection, new phone, change of address, voter registration, and driver's license; I also had to quit my old job, figure out how to get my stuff in San Francisco, and move it up here. My to do list was long, not fun. I complicated this by pursuing the job with the Alaska Marine Highway. Before I started, I needed a physical, drug test, food servers license, alcohol servers license, transportation workers identity card, and a Marine Mariner's Certificate including medical clearance approved by the United States Coast Guard. I needed them in order, and the process took ten weeks to complete. I took a temporary job to make ends meet.

As I finish writing this book, I've accepted the job with the Alaska Marine Highway System. I have all my paperwork and licenses to work on a ship. It cost $782 and took ten weeks. Orientation and training start next week. I am excited to be starting a new job. I will see Alaska and get paid to do so. I am sitting in my new apartment, nothing special, but I know I made the right decision. It took ten weeks to write the first draft, and it will take months to edit it. The editing will be done at sea. This ends my journey from San Francisco, California, to Ketchikan, Alaska, but the real story has just begun. That is the story of my life.

From Ketchikan, Alaska, with love and a story.

Steven A. Harrison
September 14, 2021

PART TWO

Pictorial Guide

The night before I left San Francisco, California, June 10, 2021.

Training for a ride in the Marin Headlands, May 2021.

Day 1, June 11, 2021, at about 9 am. This is the first place I stopped to charge my battery.

Day 1, June 11, 2021. This is the second place I charged my battery.

Day 2, June 12, 2021.
Fort Ross, California.

Day 1, June 11, 2021. I spent
the night in Bodega Bay, California. Started ride at 387 Ellis
St. San Francisco, California.
72.7 miles, elevation
2,736 feet.

Borrowing electricity from
the visitor's center. Day 2,
June 12, 2021. Rest stop
to charge my battery for
an hour in Stewarts Point,
California.

Day 2, June 12, 2021. Gualala Campground—$5 for a spot by the river. 59.4 total miles Elevation gain 2,221 feet.

Day 3, June 13, 2021. Charging battery while eating breakfast in Point Arena, California. Behind this café is a cow pasture leading to the lighthouse. This is where I was followed by 30 cows for half an hour as I hiked out to the lighthouse.

Day 3, June 13, 2021. Elk, California. The roadside library where I picked up *The Girl with the Dragon Tattoo*.

Day 3, June 13, 2021. Albion, California. Ran out of electricity eight miles from the destination. I stopped to charge my battery and play nine holes of golf.

Night 3, June 13, 2021. Russian Gulch Campground. My four-man tent with no rainfly on a rainy night. Threw the tent and makeshift rainfly away in the morning. 53.7 miles, elevation 2,677 feet.

Day 4, June 14, 2021. Fort Bragg, California. Stopped at a bike shop for new tires for Burley Bee Trailer. Charging bike at the coffee shop.

Day 4, June 14, 2021. Westport, California. Stopped at the local RV campsite for the night. Pitched my tiny two-man tent between two monster RVs. 26.3 miles, elevation 1,309 feet.

Day 5, June 15, 2021. Leggett, California. Charging battery at Peg's "Don't Ever Not Stop."

Day 5, June 15, 2021. Garberville, California. Stopped early due to a temperature of 106 degrees Fahrenheit. 53.2 miles, elevation 5,607 feet.

Day 6, June 16, 2021. Redcrest, California. I stopped for donuts and coffee next door to the post office—no place to charge in Redcrest.

Day 6, June 16, 2021. Old Redwood Highway, California. This is off Highway 101 in Mendocino. Stopped to use mother nature's bathroom.

Day 6, June 16, 2021. Humboldt Bay Wildlife Refuge, California. After looking for a place to charge my bike in Fortuna, California, and being shut down (the second most unfriendly city I came across for an e-biker), I rode on without any power to the wildlife refuge. There I met the friendliest rangers, and they let me charge my bike and take a nap in their beautiful park.

Day 6, June 16, 2021. Redwood Coast Cabins and RV Resort in Eureka, California. After 97 miles, I entered a private campground, and the ladies who worked there were some of the nicest, most helpful people I have ever met. I was dead tired, and their hospitality was heaven-sent—three thumbs up for service above and beyond the call of duty. 97.1 miles, elevation 6,810 feet.

Day 7, June 17, 2021. Orick, California. The bike trailer hitch broke, and I pulled into town looking for some parts to repair the trailer.

Day 7, June 17, 2021. Prairie Creek Redwoods State Park, Northern California. One of the smaller trees in the park.

Day 7, June 17, 2021. Prairie Creek Redwoods State Park, Northern California. Highly recommend this secondary road through the park. Incredibly beautiful.

Day 7, June 17, 2021. Klamath, California. Klamath Camper Corral. Private campground. Really helpful staff. Slept like a baby on the softest grass around. 65.8 miles, elevation 2,877 feet.

Day 8, June 18, 2021. Crescent City, California. Compared to the world-famous lumberjack, my bike and trailer seem small.

Day 8, June 18, 2021. Oregon State Line. Milestone achieved.

Day 8, June 18, 2021. Brookings, Oregon. Metal shop
in Brookings, getting my
bike trailer fixed. 51.1 miles,
elevation 1,693 feet.

Day 8, June 18, 2021.
Brookings, Oregon. One
of the most awe-inspir-
ing nights and fantastic
sunsets I have ever
seen. Humbled; nothing
less than spiritual.

Day 9, June 19, 2021. Oregon Coast State Park. Just one of many little parks along the Oregon Coast that I pulled into to rest and charge my battery in the bathroom.

Day 9, June 19, 2021. Five miles south of Humbug State Park, Oregon Coast. I bought a couple of Gatorades, some chocolate, and SweetTarts from a T-Rex. 48.9 miles, elevation 2,310 feet.

Day 10, June 20, 2021. Bandon, Oregon. One of my most creative charging sites. The abandoned weigh station on the outskirts of Bannon. Saw an electrical outlet and it was live. Trucks started to stop at the weigh station because they thought I worked there with my fluorescent green vest on. I stayed for an hour.

Day 10, June 20, 2021. Bandon, Oregon. A one-hour long conversation with a bike shop owner. No parts, but a great source of information.

Day 10, June 20, 2021. Coos Bay, Oregon. After running out of electricity six miles from town, I entered the least friendly city for e-bikers. I spent two hours looking for a place to charge. I ended up giving up and leaving town on human power and got a motel room north of Coos Bay. 62.2 miles, elevation 1,818 feet.

Day 10, June 20, 2021. North Bend, Oregon. Stayed in a little motel a couple of blocks from this city marker. After a 62-mile ride in 90-degree heat, I paid $75 for a room and was asleep within an hour. The last 12 miles of my ride were without electricity.

Day 11, June 21, 2021. Honeyman State Park, Oregon. After bike trailer troubles all day, I set up camp, unhitched the trailer, and had fun touring around the area: great place to stop, lots of fun at Honeyman State Park, Oregon.

Day 11, June 21, 2021. Honeyman State Park, Oregon. The hiker/biker campsite was very isolated from the rest of the campground. I ended up charging my bike at a visitors' center in the middle of the park. 42.5 miles, elevation 1,184 feet.

Day 11, June 21, 2021. Honeyman State Park, Oregon. Stopped early and enjoyed the day swimming.

Day 12, June 22, 2021. Near Heceto Lighthouse, Oregon. Taking advantage of free electricity.

Day 12, June 22, 2021. Waldport, Oregon. Charging my bike while eating lunch at the local Mexican restaurant.

Day 12, June 22, 2021. South Beach, Oregon. Great hiker/biker campsite with charging facilities on site.

Day 12, June 22, 2021. South Beach Campground, Oregon. Some great trails through the campgrounds and surrounding areas. 51.1 miles, elevation 1,509 feet.

Day 13, June 23, 2021. Pacific City, Oregon. Tiny city park in Pacific City about a quarter mile from the city campground, where I ate Bugles and Gatorade.

Day 13, June 23, 2021. Pacific Beach Campground, Oregon. Soft grass to sleep on and very friendly, helpful camp hosts. When I arrived, my battery was dead, and they got me all set up. 50.4 miles, elevation 1,946 feet.

Day 14, June 24, 2021. Kelly's Marina, Nehalem Bay, Oregon. One of the best decisions of my trip was an unplanned stop at Kelly's. I had a great time and ate crab. I met some great people and camped overnight. Rating ten out of ten for friendly, clean amenities and food. Perfect day and night. 43 miles, elevation 620 feet.

Day 15, June 25, 2021. Northern Oregon coast.
Above the clouds, I could not resist stopping to take
in the view.

Day 15, June 25, 2021. Nehalem, Oregon. I stopped for breakfast and a quick charge.

Day 15, June 25, 2021. Fort Stevens, Astoria, Oregon. Hiker/biker site with electricity to charge my bicycle. 45 miles, elevation 1,795 feet.

Day 15, June 25, 2021. Near Seaside, Oregon. Convenience store and RV Park. I paid the proprietor $5 to sit and charge my e-bike for two hours and met Jenny (schoolteacher) from Chattanooga, Tennessee.

Day 16, June 26, 2021. Bruce-port County Campground, Washington. Stopped early due to severe heat in Washington State. 48.4 miles, elevation 2,329 feet.

Day 17, June 27, 2021. Early morning sunrise South Bend, Washington.

Day 17, June 27, 2021. Sylvia Lake, Montesano, Washington. Incredible day and park. Met Kim, who made me dinner and took this picture. 37.8 miles, elevation 2,054 feet.

Day 17, June 27, 2021. Lake Sylvia State Park, Montesano, Washington. A truly wonderful little park and a mountain lake. I had a fabulous day avoiding the heat in the lake.

Day 18, June 28, 2021. Schafer State Park, Washington. Beat the heat for an hour while I charged my battery.

Day 18, June 28, 2021. Potlatch State Park Campground, Washington. I rode 52 miles; it was 108 degrees when I set up my campsite. I was delirious with heat exhaustion and dehydration. This is what I drank in one and a half hours after arriving. I had to lie in a small creek behind my site to cool off. It was 118 degrees in Seattle, which was less than 50 miles from my campsite. 51.6 miles, elevation 919 feet.

Day 19, June 29, 2021. Dosewallips State Park, Washington. Charging bike and having lunch.	Day 19, June 29, 2021. Quilcene, Washington. I stopped to rest for a while in the shade. It was hot. Very hot.

Day 19, June 29, 2021. Lake Leland County Campground, Washington. The weather made me do it. Short day, very hot, went swimming instead of riding. 46.1 miles, elevation 1,437 feet.

Day 20, June 30, 2021. Port Townsend, Washington. Boarding the Coupeville Ferry in Port Townsend. Short crossing over the Puget Sound.

Day 20, June 30, 2021. Deception Pass State Park, Cranberry Lake Campground, Washington. Beautiful camp-ground but a very isolated hiker/biker site. I charged the bike in the bathroom and the snack bar kiosk. 49.9 miles, elevation 1,663 feet.

Day 21, July 1, 2021. Near Edison, Wash-ington. Beautiful land; had to stop and take a picture of a rooster.

Day 21, July 1, 2021. Larrabee State Park, Washington. Highway 11, about 20 miles from Bellingham, Washington. I charged the bike's battery at the ranger station. 40.2 miles, elevation 1,171 feet.

Day 23, July 3, 2021. Blaine, Washington. Heading to the Canadian Border to chat with the Mounties. 31.5 miles, elevation 522 feet.

Day 23, July 3, 2021. Peace Arch State Park, Canada. Whoops, I entered Canada by mistake. (Ok, it was intentional, but I can't admit to breaking and entering a country in print, can I?)

Day 24, July 4, 2021, Birch Bay, Washington. Ain't that America? Little pink houses for you and me.

Day 25, July 5, 2021. Birch Bay State Park, Washington. A beautiful sunset to end a simple day.

Day 25, July 5, 2021. Birch Bay State Park, Birch Bay, Washington. As soon as the people left, the animals came back. 7.9 miles, elevation 12 feet.

Day 25, July 5, 2021. Birch Bay State Park, Washington. Charging the battery before I returned to Bellingham to board the ferry.

Day 26, July 6, 2021. Larrabee State Park, Washington. Entrance to the rocky little beach. Popular place.

Day 27, July 7, 2021. Bellingham, Washington. On my way to the Alaska Marine Highway System ferry.

Day 27, July 7, 2021. The MV Matanuska Ferry to Ketchikan, Alaska.

Day 28, July 9, 2021. Downtown Ketchikan, Alaska, two hours after I arrived in the state.

Ward Lake, Ketchikan, Alaska.

Day 28, July 9, 2021. Ketchikan, Alaska. The end of my journey—Perseverance Trailhead. Ketchikan, Alaska. Never give up on your dreams.

PART THREE

TIPS for E-BIKE TOURING

What I would have done differently.

You learn as travel on your journey through life. Sometimes, you can stop and change plans. Other times, you regret a left turn when everyone said go right. You live with the consequences because it is impossible to change history. This section is a simple discourse on things I would do differently given time, money, or opportunity.

Solar Panels

I did the research, listened to naysayers. I saw solar panel systems that worked. My trip was during a heatwave that spanned the West Coast. I experienced exceptionally dry, hot weather from California to Washington State. It was abnormal even in summertime. A solar panel is a game-changer. It would have simplified my ride. Would it make the journey better? Open for discussion. It would simplify the journey, and they work. Finding a place to charge can be daunting. Conclusion: Solar panels on an e-bike work, so spend the time and money.

Locks and Chains

I left my bike unattended for hours. I worried when I left my bike alone. It is hard to relax and enjoy yourself when you are worried about your bike. The most advanced lock on the market can be broken. Anyone determined to steal your bike can. Bike locks keep honest people honest. They prevent joy rides. A bike thief can break any lock. A diamond bit Sawzall or grinder will cut through anything on the market. I threw out my four-pound U-lock on the third day of the trip. I bought a light cable lock. Carrying the extra weight is not worth it.

Leave the Weight at Home

Do not carry extra weight. Four pounds over 1,700 miles is a lot of weight to carry. A quarter-pound cable lock provided the same amount of protection. The best protection is a GPS locator and common sense. As e-bikes have become more popular, so have GPS bike alarms. For high-end touring bikes, the cost is well worth the peace of mind. The bike I rode cost $4,000, so insurance and an electronic locator is a good idea. I would invest in an electronic alarm.

Recharging Systems

The solar panel system works. It will also work on overcast days but not efficiently. It would have worked every day for 28 days. I spent a lot of time and energy finding charging locations. I rented hotel rooms, which cost hundreds of dollars. If I had a solar recharging system, it would have saved time and money. There are external battery chargers, and there are multiple battery systems. If you want an easy ride, research and invest in multiple battery systems and chargers. I met a couple that used a gas-powered generator attached to a bike trailer. They charged multiple batteries and never needed to stop and recharge. I thought it was overkill, but it worked for them.

Touring Bikes

I love my Specialized Vado; it is not a touring bike. There are touring e-bikes, and more are coming. The bicycle companies will supply the demand. One advantage an e-touring-bike has over my Vado is two-batteries. There are also bikes where you can charge one battery while using the other. My e-bike did not allow this. The battery is built into the bike; switching it would be easy, except you need new software to use the battery. There are touring bikes that allow you to unplug one battery and plug in another. Standardized batteries have external charging systems. Charging one battery while you are riding is viable, especially with solar. It might not be efficient, but using alternating batteries and charging both at night would be simple.

Battery Efficiency with a Trailer

I spent as much time charging my bike as riding it. I would ride three hours, just getting into a rhythm, then need to stop and charge the battery. Using a trailer carrying 65 pounds of equipment ran down the battery quickly. Lost efficiency due to weight should be minimized. Train for your ride with the additional weight. Running a lithium-ion battery to zero is not an optimal situation. When my battery showed 10%, I had none, the bike shut itself off to conserve the battery core. I did not train with a trailer attached; I had no idea what the battery system would do. Lower efficiency pulling a trailer cannot be dismissed. I misjudged battery usage several times. Investigate your battery management while you are close to home and not out in the middle of nowhere. If you are going to use a trailer, train with the trailer attached.

Judge Your Abilities

Know your bike and your abilities. I trained for months, I varied my rides and my training techniques. I used two different bikes and evaluated the trailer on both bikes. I chose the faster road bike for my tour. It has a slightly bigger engine but a smaller battery. Make sure you know your equipment and train using one bicycle. I spent hours in the gym strengthening my arms, back, and lungs before I left. I recommend you do the same. Riding every day is not enough. Spend an hour a day on the Stairmaster, lifecycle, and treadmill. Hit the weights for upper body conditioning. This is not a necessity, but a wise move. Your trip will tax your whole body, not just your legs, ass, and lungs.

Getting in Shape

An e-bike will take the physical stress off your ride. It will make mountains scalable and headwinds livable. Do not kid yourself; touring is not a day in the park. You must ride your bike and stay alert for obstacles and road variables. You will encounter obstacles along the way. You need a minimum of physical conditioning before you tour on an e-bike. Think of it this way; I did the same ride on an e-bike I did on a regular bike when I was 18 years old. Getting on an e-bike allows you to feel like an 18-year-old again, but if you are not 18, you still need to be in shape to ride 10 hours a day. The e-bike takes the stress off the body but does not reduce it to zero. Get in shape before you ride.

Navigation Systems

Buy a good navigation system for your ride. It needs a separate power supply, not your phone. There are great tour biking navigation systems on the market. I did not have one. Buy a good one and leave your phone alone. I used my phone, but even the best phone system will not work in isolated mountain canyons and areas where you have cliffs on both sides. The signal cannot reach you, and your phone will automatically increase its power usage to locate a signal for you. While you are riding, the battery drains fast. Your phone might overheat as it tries to determine your location. When you need your phone, it's dead and useless. My advice: use a separate system, not your phone. Use a phone as a backup only.

USB Plug-Ins

Find an e-bike that has a USB port or buy a secondary market system. My bike does not have one. It would have been wonderful. If you use your phone for navigation, using the bike battery rather than your phone battery would be useful. You can bring a backup USB battery; I did and used it often. They are great, but if your bike has a USB charger, think how easy this would make your life on the road. I used two lights, a lantern, radio, and my phone, which all charged off of a USB port. It would help to plug your peripherals into the bike's battery.

Trailers and Spare Parts

I had trouble with my trailer hitch. I went through two sets of tires on my trailer. I passed three people touring using a trailer. Everyone else used panniers and bike bags. My touring has been camping trips. I like to unhitch my bike and be unobstructed once I set up camp. I used one of the best bike trailers available. I would use panniers rather than a trailer. You can unsnap a couple of bike bags; it is not that big of a deal.

On the third day, the trailer snapped the rear axle hitch. The steel hitch threads onto an aluminum axle, which shreds the aluminum. My trailer was not overweight but modified three inches longer in the front and nine inches in the back. This added a foot of space to my trailer. This changed the physical stress on the hitch. I am not an engineer, but common sense and construction experience tells me when you modify one part, you are asking for trouble with the others.

Physics and Stress Points

Once the stress and balance change, you end up with a Rubik's Cube of problems. You've solved one problem; another one creeps up behind you. I struggled with my trailer the whole trip. After the hitch broke, the connector broke, then the arm attached to the trailer broke, and then and then and then. My Rubik's Cube of problems was my own making. The company makes trailers for children; I take blame for my trailer problems because I modified it past the originally intended size. It got me to Alaska. It was great when working properly.

Panniers Explained

I recommend panniers and bike bags for two reasons. One, they are less stressful on the bike. Two, wind resistance is less. You will travel lighter. I went on a tune-up ride before Alaska. I carried way too much. I rode from sea level over a 7,000-foot mountain, regretting the extra weight. I reduced the weight 40% from my tune-up ride. I still carried too much. I got away with it because I was using a bike trailer. You can carry more in a trailer. It makes overpacking easy. I brought luxuries I did not need, like a two-man tent, laptop, and peripherals. I should have taken an iPad and a one-man tent.

Engine Size Matters

There is new technology hitting the e-bike market. Some good, some bad, and all marketed like it is the best thing around. Select an e-bike from a company that has been around for a while. Cannondale, Specialized, Giant, Trek, etc., are good bike brands. There are a lot of newcomers to the party. The issue with these companies is not one of good or bad. It is a problem with service and parts for your bike. Not all bike shops will service e-bikes. Be aware that what you buy today might not be serviceable in the future.

High Technology

E-bikes are modern technology. They are part bike, part electronics and high technology, including battery management systems, charging technologies, electric controllers, navigation systems, GPS, etc. This is not your grandfather's beach cruiser that needs a little chain oil once every ten years. A good e-bike is going to have special parts, a computer system, and a battery management system. Your weekend warrior will be hard-pressed to figure these out.

Getting Service for Your E-Bike

If you buy an e-bike from a bike shop, no matter how cool it is, how well built, it is going to need service by an e-bike technician. E-bikes are complicated machinery. Changing a tire on a hub-mounted e-bike can be daunting. Breaks in a wire can be difficult to solve without the right equipment. Take care when you buy a bike, as problems are exasperated when you cannot find a mechanic. I am on my fourth e-bike, so I learned the hard way. Not every bike shop will work on your bike.

E-Bike DIY Kits

I built my first e-bike from a kit. It was a front hub trike, modified extensively. I rebuilt the brake system three times, replacing brake pads every three months. I broke spokes like matchsticks. I bought new forks. I bought new handlebars. I bought metal baskets and welded mounts. Things kept breaking. A year and a half later, this super cool 30 mph trike broke its back axle. It took three months to get a new axle. I was so frustrated waiting for the part, I bought a store-built e-bike.

Mid Drive, Front Hub or Rear Hub Explained

The Fuji Sanibel was a rear-hub pedal-assist e-bike. A beach cruiser model. I raced the bike up and down the hills of San Francisco, and it rode like a tank. It took a beating and kept right on ticking. The brakes went out. I replaced the brake pads twelve times in eight months. Rebuilt the brake system, ended up with disc and caliper brakes. I had two sets of brakes on the front and back. The chain broke, and spokes busted. I learned an e-bike is not a bicycle. The speed of movement creates torque on the frame, spokes, wheels, brakes, tires, and chain. The faster you ride, the more torque you create; things break with prolonged tension created by torque.

E-Bike Frame Mechanics

Bicycles are designed for a certain speed. When you add an electric engine, you have to think about torque and what it does to a bicycle. When you buy an e-bike, make sure it was engineered as an e-bike. You need oversized brakes with a cutoff switch built-in, designed well. You need super strong wheels, rims, spokes, and hubs designed for speeds in excess of 25 mph. Your average bicycle is designed for maximum speeds of 12 to 15 mph. When you double that, you more than double the torque. Problems will quadruple; catastrophic failure is possible. Losing brakes is bad, but having the engine cutoff fail in city traffic is deadly.

Safety Equipment and Information

Always wear a helmet. If you have an accident at 25 mph, you are going to get hurt. The faster the speed, the less reaction time you have. Your braking distance increases. Make sure your brakes work well and that you pay attention to what is in front of you; your life could depend on it. E-bikes on the market look super cool; they work great, have powerful engines, and have terrible brakes, so be careful. Spend the extra money on a good helmet.

Electric Motorcycle vs. E-Bike

There are bikes with large, heavy batteries, the frame designed for speeds over 15 mph and extra weight. The most dangerous are throttle-mounted e-bikes. These lead to complacency, careless riding. If you want an electric motorcycle, go buy one. If you buy a throttle-mounted e-bike, buy a motorcycle helmet. You are going to need it. I am not against hybrids or throttle-mounted electric motorcycles. I am saying be careful, as they are fast and can be dangerous if not ridden properly. They are motorcycles, not bicycles.

Modifications

Every e-bike I own had repairs and modifications. Modifications to an e-bike are not cheap or easy. Do not buy a cheap e-bike thinking that it will last for years. You will get what you pay for. A more powerful engine also means more repairs and maintenance. Modifications should only be done with safety in mind. Making it go faster is fun but comes at a cost. Make sure you engineer modifications accordingly. Do not modify your e-bike past the speed it was designed for. Modifying an e-bike to go 45 mph is possible, but without increasing the strength of the other parts it is extremely dangerous.

Cost of E-bikes and Batteries

Balance the cost and lifespan desired. Repairs and maintenance must be factored in. Spending more does not mean fewer repairs. With any new market, there are companies capitalizing on hype. Be careful if you plan to tour the country on an e-bike. I rode 600 miles between certified Specialized mechanics. Learn everything about your bike before you travel.

My bike was tuned and repaired before I left for Alaska. I had zero mechanical problems on my trip. I had problems with my bicycle trailer. As discussed earlier, I take responsibility for the trailer problems. Modifying things to my liking without regard to engineering creates problems. You learn what will work and what will not.

The Most Important Thing You Need

The most important thing you need before any adventure is a good attitude. Unexpected things will happen. That is life. You can plan everything; it will inevitably go wrong. When this happens; stop, take a deep breath, say "oh well, that did not work." Focus on solutions; do not waste your energy on the problem. If you are human, you will find a way to fix the problem. It is part of life. Roll with the punches; do not sweat the little things. If you get a flat tire or break a spoke or brake pad, just fix it. You can do anything you put your mind to. Don't worry about what "might happen." If I worried about all the "what ifs," I would never have left San Francisco. Plan your trip with a margin of error. Budget your money with wiggle room. Add a few days or hours to your timeline. If you turn left, you might find something interesting or beautiful. Just do it. If you plan your trip precisely, you won't smell the roses. Slow down and enjoy your journey, and that is the journey of life.

The end.

EPILOGUE

Perseverance:
An E-Bike Journey to Alaska

I finished this book on September 14, 2021; since that time, much has changed in my life. I went to orientation for the Alaska Marine Highway System on September 21, 2021. They put me to work shortly thereafter. I am now working full time on the ferry system. The work is hard, sometimes long hours and little sleep. It is not unusual to work 96 hours a week. I enjoy traveling to new places, seeing new things, and riding my bike in new towns.

I rented a nicer apartment, bought a kayak, made new friends. I worked all winter in the shipyard, fitting out an Alaska Marine Highway Ferry for sea trials and an Annual Certificate of Inspection. It made my first Alaskan winter go by quickly. I spent eight weeks in class training over the past year, and I have an able seaman rating from the United States Coast Guard. It took sixteen months. I am happy, healthy, and grounded in Alaska. I plan to stay, to look for property and a permanent residence. I write a blog about living in Alaska on Medium.com. Living in Alaska provides me with ample writing opportunities. Alaska has been good for me; the positives outweigh the negatives by volume.

I came to see my fiftieth state, and since I arrived, I have visited the following cities, towns, and villages: Ketchikan, Wrangell, Petersburg, Juneau, Whittier, Cordova, Valdez, Anchorage, Kodiak, Chenega Bay, Tatitlek, Port Lions, Ouzinkie, Soldotna, Seldovia, Seward, Homer, Yakutat, Haines, Skagway, Angoon, Hoonah, Tenakee Springs, Pelican, Sitka, Kake, Coffman Cove, Craig, Klawock, Saxman, Hollis, and Metlakatla. I have seen the Iditarod, whales, dolphins, eagles, orcas, seals, bears, wolves, and my favorite, sea otters. I have skied, kayaked, mountain biked, and fished for salmon. I still have an extensive to-do list, but I am living in Alaska.

From Ketchikan, Alaska, with love and a story.

Steve Harrison
December 30, 2022

ABOUT ATMOSPHERE PRESS

Founded in 2015, Atmosphere Press was built on the principles of Honesty, Transparency, Professionalism, Kindness, and Making Your Book Awesome. As an ethical and author-friendly hybrid press, we stay true to that founding mission today.

If you're a reader, enter our giveaway for a free book here:

SCAN TO ENTER
BOOK GIVEAWAY

If you're a writer, submit your manuscript for consideration here:

SCAN TO SUBMIT
MANUSCRIPT

And always feel free to visit Atmosphere Press and our authors online at atmospherepress.com. See you there soon!

ABOUT the AUTHOR

Photo by **Sage Smiley**

STEVEN HARRISON is a graduate of the University of California, Santa Barbara. He has been an Accountant, Mortgage Broker, Financial Analyst, Development Associate, and is now a Deckhand on the Alaska Marine Highway. He writes a blog at medium.com/@stevenharrison2016 and can be found at Quora.com as well. He currently resides in Ketchikan, Alaska.

You can also find Steven at stevenharrisonwrites.com.

Milton Keynes UK
Ingram Content Group UK Ltd.
UKHW010913080424
440801UK00004B/377